SELLING YOUR CRAFTS ONLINE

with Etsy, eBay®, and Pinterest

Michael Miller

800 East 96th Street,
Indianapolis, Indiana 46240 USA

SELLING YOUR CRAFTS ONLINE
WITH ETSY, EBAY, AND PINTEREST

COPYRIGHT © 2013 BY QUE PUBLISHING

ISBN-13: 978-0-7897-5032-7
ISBN-10: 0-7897-5032-5

Library of Congress Cataloging-in-Publication data is on file.

Printed in the United States of America

First Printing: October 2012

TRADEMARKS

WARNING AND DISCLAIMER

BULK SALES

Que Publishing offers excellent discounts on this book when ordered in quantity for bulk purchases or special sales. For more information, please contact

U.S. Corporate and Government Sales
1-800-382-3419
corpsales@pearsontechgroup.com

For sales outside the United States, please contact

International Sales
international@pearsoned.com

EDITOR-IN-CHIEF
Greg Wiegand

EXECUTIVE EDITOR
Rick Kughen

DEVELOPMENT EDITOR
Rick Kughen

MANAGING EDITOR
Sandra Schroeder

SENIOR PROJECT EDITOR
Tonya Simpson

INDEXER
Cheryl Lenser

PROOFREADER
Sarah Kearns

TECHNICAL EDITOR
Todd Meister

PUBLISHING COORDINATORS
Cindy Teeters
Romny French

BOOK DESIGNER
Anne Jones

COMPOSITOR
Trina Wurst

CONTENTS AT A GLANCE

Introduction 1

PART I: GETTING READY TO SELL
1 Planning for Success 5
2 Setting the Right Price 21
3 Putting Together a Successful Listing 31
4 Taking Powerful Pictures 43

PART II: SELLING ONLINE
5 Deciding Where to Sell Online 63
6 Selling on Etsy 91
7 Selling on eBay 111
8 Selling on Your Own Website 133

PART III: RUNNING A SUCCESSFUL CRAFTS BUSINESS
9 Handling Online Payments 147
10 Shipping Your Merchandise 157
11 Serving Your Customers 171
12 Managing Your Inventory 179
13 Promoting Your Business with Pinterest 187
14 Other Ways to Promote Your Business 203
15 Measuring Your Success 213
Index 225

TABLE OF CONTENTS

INTRODUCTION 1

PART I: GETTING READY TO SELL

1 PLANNING FOR SUCCESS 5

So You Want to Sell Your Crafts Online 6

What Sells Online—and What Doesn't 8
    Crafts You Probably Shouldn't Sell Online 8
    What Types of Crafts *Do* Sell Well Online? 10

Why Planning Is a Good Idea 12
    What a Business Plan Does for You 12
    Things You Need to Plan 12

How Much Planning Do You Need to Do? 13
    The Occasional Seller 13
    The Growing Seller 14
    The Full-Time Seller 15

Putting Together a No-Frills Business Plan 15
    Before You Plan: Think Things Through 15
    Parts of a Successful Business Plan 17
    Talking Through Your Plan 18
    Writing the Plan 20

You've Planned the Plan: Now What? 20

2 SETTING THE RIGHT PRICE 21

Researching the Market 22

Calculating Your Costs 23
    Calculating Materials Costs 24
    Calculating Labor Costs 24
    Calculating Selling Fees 25
    Calculating Packaging Costs 25

Calculating the Selling Price 26
    Why 4 x Costs Works 26
    Fine-Tuning Your Selling Price 27

Calculating Profit 29
    Understanding Gross and Net 29
    Are You Making Money? 29

Considering Wholesale Pricing 30

3   PUTTING TOGETHER A SUCCESSFUL LISTING 31

Writing an Attention-Grabbing Title...32
   Creating a Searchable Title...33
   Making Your Title POP 35
   Watch the Length...35

Creating a Descriptive Description...36
   Include All the Details...37
   Prioritize Your Information...39
   Stress Benefits, Not Features...39
   Use Power Words—But Avoid Superlatives...40

Add Your Personal Style...40

Don't Forget the Pictures!...41

4   TAKING POWERFUL PICTURES 43

What You Need to Take Effective Product Photos...44
   Choosing the Right Digital Camera...44
   Going Steady with a Tripod...46
   Enhancing Your Photos with Auxiliary Lighting...46
   Keeping It Plain with Photo Backgrounds...48
   Considering a Light Tent for Smaller Items...49
   Fixing the Flaws with Photo Editing Software...51

How to Take Great Product Photos...52

Working with Lighting...52

Tips for Improving Your Product Photos...54
   Center the Item...54
   Make It Large...54
   Shoot at an Angle...55
   Shoot Multiple Photos...55
   Avoid Glare...56
   Accessorize Your Photos...56

Shooting Different Types of Crafts...57
   Shooting Clear or Translucent Glass...57
   Shooting Opaque Glass and Jewelry...58
   Shooting Wood Items...58
   Shooting Clothing...58
   Scanning Flat and Small Items...60

Editing Your Photos—Digitally...60

PART II: SELLING ONLINE

5   DECIDING WHERE TO SELL ONLINE 63

Selling on Dedicated Online Craft Marketplaces 64

Etsy 64

Artbreak 66

ArtFire 66

Artful Home 68

Artist Rising 69

Artspan 69

Bonanza 70

Craft Is Art 70

Crobbies 71

Funky Finds 72

Handmade Artists Shop 73

Handmade Catalog 74

Hyena Cart 74

Made It Myself 75

ShopHandmade 76

Yessy 76

Zibbet 77

Selling on General Online Marketplaces 78

eBay 78

Craigslist 79

eCRATER 80

Ruby Lane 81

SilkFair 82

Comparing the Top Online Marketplaces 83

Examining Important Factors 84

Type of Site 84

Size and Traffic 85

Fees 85

Comparing the Big Two: Etsy vs. eBay 86

Selling on Your Own Website 88

Settling on a Site—Or Two 89

6   SELLING ON ETSY 91

Getting to Know Etsy 92

What Can You Sell on Etsy? 93

How Does Etsy Work? 94

What It Costs to Sell on Etsy 96
    Etsy Shop Fees 97
    Listing Fees 97
    Transaction Fees 97
    Payment Processing Fees 98
    Paying Etsy 98

Signing Up for an Etsy Account 98

Setting Up Your Etsy Shop 100
    Creating Your Shop 100
    Customizing Your Shop 101

Creating a New Item Listing 102
    Starting a New Listing 102
    Editing an Item Listing 105
    Renewing a Listing 105
    Deactivating a Listing 105

Getting Paid 105
    Etsy Direct Checkout 106
    PayPal 106
    Other Payment Methods 107

Managing Your Etsy Sales 107

Tips for Making More Money on Etsy 108
    Spruce Up Your Shop 108
    Create a Powerful Cover Image 108
    List More to Sell More 109
    List or Renew Daily 110
    Make Sure You Tag Your Items 110
    Pack Promotionally 110
    Increase Your Feedback by Buying on Etsy 110

7   SELLING ON EBAY 111

Understanding eBay 112
    Size Matters 112
    Who Sells on eBay? 113
    eBay for Crafters 113

How to Sell on eBay 114
    Auction Listings 114
    Auctions with the Buy It Now Option 115
    Fixed Price Listings 116
    eBay Store Listings 116
    Which Type of Listing Is Best for You? 117

Understanding eBay's Fees 117

Signing Up for eBay 120

Listing an Item for Sale 121
    Creating an Auction Listing 121
    Adding the Buy It Now Option 123
    Creating a Fixed-Price Listing 124

Opening an eBay Store 125
    What Is an eBay Store? 125
    Benefits of Opening Your Own eBay Store 126
    The Costs of Running an eBay Store 127
    Choosing the Right Subscription Level 127
    Setting Up Your Store 128
    Listing Merchandise for Sale 128
    Customizing and Managing Your Store 128

Getting Paid 129

Managing Your eBay Activity 129

Tips for Maximizing Your eBay Sales 130
    Pick the Right Category 130
    Enhance Your Listing Descriptions 130
    Choose a Longer Listing 132
    Don't Forget the Pictures 132
    Avoid Deadbeats 132

8 SELLING ON YOUR OWN WEBSITE **133**

Building an Online Store—What's Involved? 134
    The Components of an Ecommerce Website 134
    Different Ways to Build a Store 136
    How Much Does It Cost? 137

Pros and Cons of Running Your Own Website 138
    Pros of Running Your Own Online Store 138
    Cons of Running Your Own Online Store 139

Does an Online Store Make Sense for Your Crafts? 140

Choosing a Hosting Service 141
    Features to Look For 142
    Comparing Prices 144

PART III: RUNNING A SUCCESSFUL CRAFTS BUSINESS

9 HANDLING ONLINE PAYMENTS 147

Examining Your Options 148

Accepting Cash, Checks, and Money Orders 149
    Cash 149
    C.O.D. 149
    Personal Checks 150
    Money Orders and Cashier's Checks 151
    Credit Cards 151

Examining the Big Payment Processing Services 152
    PayPal 152
    Google Checkout 154
    Checkout by Amazon 155

10 SHIPPING YOUR MERCHANDISE 157

Choosing a Shipping Method 158
    U.S. Postal Service 159
    FedEx 161
    UPS 161
    Other Shipping Companies 162

Calculating Shipping and Handling Fees 162
    Working with Flat Fees 163
    Determining the Handling Charge 163

Packing Your Items 163
    Picking the Right Shipping Container 164
    How to Pack 165
    One Size Doesn't Fit All 166
    How to Seal the Package 167
    Creating the Shipping Label 168
    To Insure or Not Insure? 169

Shipping Internationally 169

11 SERVICING YOUR CUSTOMERS 171

Answering Customer Questions 172

Managing Post-Sale Correspondence 173

Handling Customer Complaints 174
    Listing Your Terms of Service 175
    Guaranteeing Your Merchandise 175

12   MANAGING YOUR INVENTORY..179

How to Manage Your Craft Inventory..180

Build in Advance or Build to Order?.......................................180

Maintaining Adequate Inventory Levels.................................181

Tracking Inventory...182

Managing Inventory Across Multiple Marketplaces....................182

Benefits of Offering Items on Multiple Sites..........................183

Drawbacks of Offering Items Across Multiple Sites................184

Multi-Site Inventory Management Solutions..........................185

13   PROMOTING YOUR BUSINESS WITH PINTEREST.................187

Getting to Know Pinterest...188

Using Pinterest..189

Signing Up for a Pinterest Account.....................................189

How Pins Work...189

What Happens When You Click a Pin..................................190

Understanding Pinboards...192

Following Other Users...193

Pinning Your Item Listings to Pinterest..................................194

Pinning an Etsy Listing..196

Pinning an eBay Listing...196

Making Your Pin a Gift Item..196

Using Pinterest to Promote Your Crafts..................................198

Pin Those Listings—Regularly...198

Create Customer-Focused Pinboards..................................198

Think Visually—But Don't Forget the Description..................200

Link Pinterest to Your Website or Shop...............................200

Link Pinterest to Other Social Networks.............................201

14   OTHER WAYS TO PROMOTE YOUR BUSINESS.....................203

Promoting via Facebook..204

Promoting in Your Facebook News Feed..............................204

Creating a Facebook Business Page....................................205

Promoting via Twitter...206

Promoting on Etsy...208

Etsy Coupon Codes..208

Etsy Search Ads..209

Etsy on Sale..210

Promoting in an Online Crafts Mall...210

Promoting with Google AdWords...211

15 MEASURING YOUR SUCCESS..213

Measuring Traffic..214

Understanding Web Analytics..214

Tracking Etsy Traffic..215

Tracking eBay Traffic..216

Tracking Traffic on Your Own Site...216

Measuring Sales..217

Understanding Sales and Revenues..218

Tracking Etsy Sales...218

Tracking eBay Sales..219

Measuring Profits...220

Calculating Gross Profit per Item...220

Calculating Net Profit for Your Business...................................223

How Do You Define Success?..223

INDEX..225

ABOUT THE AUTHOR

Michael Miller is a successful and prolific author with a reputation for practical advice and technical accuracy and an unerring empathy for the needs of his readers.

Mr. Miller has written more than 100 best-selling books over the past two decades. His books include *My Pinterest, Sams Teach Yourself eBay in 10 Minutes, Making a Living from Your eBay Business, Absolute Beginner's Guide to eBay, Absolute Beginner's Guide to Computer Basics,* and *Selling Online 2.0: Migrating from eBay to Amazon, Craigslist, and Your Own E-Commerce Website.* He is known for his casual, easy-to-read writing style and his practical, real-world advice—as well as his ability to explain a wide variety of complex topics to an everyday audience.

You can email Mr. Miller directly at crafts@molehillgroup.com. His website is located at www.molehillgroup.com.

DEDICATION

To all five of my wonderful grandchildren: Collin, Alethia, Hayley, Judah, and Lael.
You make life fun.

ACKNOWLEDGMENTS

Thanks to the usual suspects at Que Publishing, including but not limited to Greg Wiegand, Rick Kughen, Tonya Simpson, and technical editor Todd Meister.

WE WANT TO HEAR FROM YOU!

As the reader of this book, *you* are our most important critic and commentator. We value your opinion and want to know what we're doing right, what we could do better, what areas you'd like to see us publish in, and any other words of wisdom you're willing to pass our way.

We welcome your comments. You can email or write to let us know what you did or didn't like about this book—as well as what we can do to make our books better.

Please note that we cannot help you with technical problems related to the topic of this book.

When you write, please be sure to include this book's title and author as well as your name and email address. We will carefully review your comments and share them with the author and editors who worked on the book.

Email: feedback@quepublishing.com

Mail: Que Publishing
            ATTN: Reader Feedback
            800 East 96th Street
            Indianapolis, IN 46240 USA

READER SERVICES

Visit our website and register this book at quepublishing.com/register for convenient access to any updates, downloads, or errata that might be available for this book.

INTRODUCTION

Crafting is a wonderful hobby, and for many a rewarding profession. After you've been at it awhile, you may start selling the crafts you make, to friends and family but also at trunk shows, sales parties, and large craft shows.

The thing is, you can also sell your crafts online. There are lots of online marketplaces that make it easy to sell your crafts and even create your own online storefront. It's pretty much as simple as shooting a few photos of your items, setting the price, and creating an item listing; after that, it's just waiting for someone to come by and purchase what you have for sale.

If you're an active crafter, you probably know some of these websites. Etsy, I'm guessing, is known to all serious craft lovers as the place to shop for handmade crafts and craft supplies. eBay also has a lot of satisfied shoppers, and there are a number of lesser-known but equally viable arts and crafts marketplaces on the web.

Well, anyplace you can buy crafts online, you can also sell them. And that's what this book is about—helping you start selling your crafts online.

Now, selling crafts online is different from selling other types of products. First of all, you probably don't consider your crafts *products*, but rather unique items you pour your heart and soul into. Fair enough. Crafts are handmade items, often one of a kind, and cannot and should not be sold in the same ways or at the same places that one would sell toilet paper or light bulbs. It's a much different process selling handmade crafts than mass-produced consumer goods.

That doesn't mean that good business principles don't apply to craft selling, because they do. In fact, the most successful craft sellers are those who possess solid business skills, do their planning in advance, and treat what others think of as a hobby as a real business. Whether you're selling one item or a hundred, you still have to present your crafts in a professional fashion, treat your customers with respect, accept all forms of payment, and pack and ship your sold items in a safe and timely manner. You know, just like a real business does.

All this applies to anyone wanting to sell their crafts online. It doesn't matter whether you're a hobbyist with just a few items to sell, someone who's already familiar with traditional craft selling, or an experienced seller who wants to expand your sales channels. *Selling Your Crafts Online* will tell you what you need to know to start selling online and become more successful at it.

I'll cover selling on Etsy and eBay, of course, as well as point out lots of other craft-selling sites you may want to consider. I'll even discuss setting up your own online craft store on your own ecommerce website, which is an option larger sellers may want to consider. And I'll provide plenty of tips and advice to make the whole online selling thing go a little smoother—and, hopefully, become a lot more profitable for you.

When you're done reading, you should know what you need to know to dip your toes into the online craft sales market. Lots of other crafters are doing it; you should be able to, too.

HOW THIS BOOK IS ORGANIZED

This book is written for any type or size of crafter who wants to get into online selling. As such, I've organized the information into three main parts, as follows:

■ **Part I, "Getting Ready to Sell,"** walks you through everything you need to do *before* you start selling. I'll discuss the value of putting together a short business plan for your craft selling, how to set the selling price for your crafts, how to put together a powerful item listing, and how to take appealing photographs of the items you want to sell. It's homework, yes, but valuable homework.

- **Part II, "Selling Online,"** gets into the nuts and bolts of the various ways to sell your crafts online. I'll discuss a variety of different websites designed for craft sellers and help you decide which of these best meet your needs. Then I'll walk you step-by-step through selling on the two largest online marketplaces for crafters, Etsy and eBay. Finally, we discuss the pros and cons of setting up your own craft-selling website—which isn't necessarily for everybody.

- **Part III, "Running a Successful Crafts Business,"** gets us into the business side of craft selling. We cover a lot of ground here, from payment processing and shipping to customer service and inventory management. You'll even learn how to promote your craft listings, using Pinterest and other Internet-based resources. Finally, I walk you through the various ways to track your sales performance—and determine if your business is successful or not.

Taken together, the 15 chapters in this book will help you set up and manage your craft sales online. Read what you need, and before long you'll be selling your handmade items online like a pro!

CONVENTIONS USED IN THIS BOOK

I hope that this book is easy enough to figure out on its own, without requiring its own instruction manual. As you read through the pages, however, it helps to know precisely how I've presented specific types of information.

WEB PAGE ADDRESSES

Because we're covering selling online, this book contains the addresses for a lot of different web pages. Technically, a web page address is supposed to start with http:// (as in http://www.molehillgroup.com). Because Internet Explorer and other web browsers automatically insert this piece of the address, however, you don't have to type it—and I haven't included it in any of the addresses in this book.

As to the accuracy of those addresses (also called URLs)—well, I've tried my best to be as accurate as possible when this book was written, in late summer 2012. Know, however, that websites come and go and specific address may change from what we have listed here. If you enter a given address and come up with a blank, try Googling the site. If you still get nothing, then that site probably closed up shop—which happens, sometimes.

SPECIAL ELEMENTS

This book also includes a few special elements that provide additional information not included in the basic text. These elements are designed to supplement the text to make your learning faster, easier, and more efficient.

TIP A *selling tip* is a piece of advice—a little trick, actually—that helps you sell online more effectively or efficiently.

NOTE A *selling note* is designed to provide information that is generally useful or interesting but not specifically essential for what you're doing at the moment.

CAUTION A *selling caution* tells you to beware of a potentially dangerous act or situation. In some cases, ignoring a caution could cause you significant problems—so pay attention to them!

LET ME KNOW WHAT YOU THINK

I always love to hear from readers. If you want to contact me, feel free to email me at crafts@molehillgroup.com. I can't promise that I'll be able to *answer* every message, but I do promise that I'll *read* each one!

And if you want to learn more about me and any new books I have cooking, check out my Molehill Group website at www.molehillgroup.com. Who knows, you might find some other books there that you would like to read.

Planning for Success

1

You make your own crafts or artwork, and you're pretty good at it, in all modesty. Maybe it's a hobby for you, maybe it's more of a full-time thing. In any case, you really enjoy what you do and you'd like to generate a little cash for your efforts, beyond what you can get from the standard craft show circuit. You've been thinking about selling your items online, but you're not quite sure how to get started.

That's why you need a plan.

Before you create a single online listing for the items you make, it helps to do a little planning. You need to think about how much money you need to invest, how much you'll spend on listings and packing materials and such, and how many sales you might make—or need to make, to cover your fixed costs. Heck, you probably need to do some research as to what online craft selling is all about—where to sell your crafts, and how.

It's all a matter of creating a roadmap for success, in the form of a short business plan that tells you what you need to do to profitably sell your crafts online.

SO YOU WANT TO SELL YOUR CRAFTS ONLINE

Many people create handmade crafts and art. For some, it's a personal thing, to display or use around the house. For others, however, it's a potential source of income; that is, you make your crafts for others to buy.

Traditionally, there have been lots of different venues for selling your handmade crafts. You can take a booth at your local arts fair, get on board the regional crafts fair circuit, even open your own gallery, if you're big enough.

Today, however, you have another option available—selling your crafts online. Lots of people are doing it. Some sell a piece at a time, others have lots of items available for sale. For some crafters, the Internet represents a significant source of income. For others, it's just a way to generate a few extra dollars they might not have had otherwise.

In any instance, the Internet can and perhaps should be a part of your sales mix. Now, you already know the various "real world" venues for selling your crafts—craft shows, arts and crafts sales parties, trunk shows, and the like. You may be less aware, however, of the various venues for online craft selling.

I like to break down all the different places you can sell online into three primary categories, as follows:

- **Craft-focused shopping sites.** These are websites, such as Etsy (shown in Figure 1.1) and ArtFire, dedicated to buying and selling crafts. Sellers post listings for the items they have for sale (often creating their own online shop or store), and sellers shop the items and buy what they like. The site facilitates the process by gathering multiple sellers all in one place and often providing payment processing options.

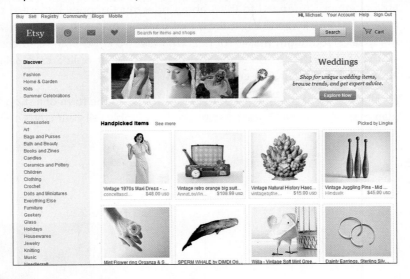

FIGURE 1.1

Etsy, a popular craft-focused shopping site.

- **General auction sites.** These are sites, typified by eBay (shown in Figure 1.2), that offer all sorts of items for sale either via online auction or at a fixed price. Like the craft-focused sites, the auction site provides a variety of support services, include payment processing; unlike the craft sites, these sites offer more than just craft items for sale—which can be both a good thing (more traffic) and a bad thing (less-focused traffic).

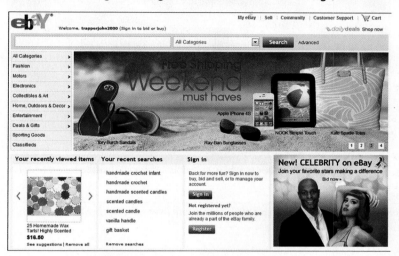

FIGURE 1.2

eBay, the most popular online auction site for crafters.

- **Your own web store.** This is an option for larger sellers only, as there's a lot more effort and cost involved. (Figure 1.3 shows a self-run website set up by a popular crafter.) Still, if you have a lot of items to sell and anticipate a high volume, it may be worth the effort.

> **NOTE** Learn more about choosing online sales venues in Chapter 5, "Deciding Where to Sell Online."

None of these venues are mutually exclusive. You can choose to sell your crafts on both Etsy and eBay, and on your own website. In fact, the more venues you utilize, the more exposure you have for your crafts—and the more exposure, the more sales you're likely to generate. Just know that managing listings on multiple sites will take more time on your part; if you're a more casual seller, it may be better to limit your efforts to one or two of the larger venues.

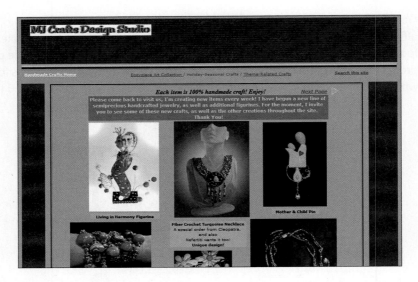

FIGURE 1.3

The Hutch with Mutch's dedicated online crafts store (www.thehutchwithmutch.com).

CAUTION Selling on multiple sites can be tricky; you don't want to sell the same unique item twice! This requires some degree of sophistication in inventory management, to keep track of items across multiple storefronts.

And don't forget, even when you go online, you can still sell your crafts out in the real world. For many craftspeople and artists, online selling merely supplements their traditional selling methods—brings in a little additional income over what they get from crafts shows and the like.

WHAT SELLS ONLINE—AND WHAT DOESN'T

When it comes to what crafts you absolutely can or can't sell online, there are no rules. In general, you can sell just about anything you can make—although, practically, some items are better suited for online selling than others.

CRAFTS YOU PROBABLY SHOULDN'T SELL ONLINE

Probably the biggest factor in determining whether or not you can sell something online is the shippability of the item. If an item is easily and inexpensively shipped, it's probably something that you can sell online. If, on the other hand, an item is too big or too heavy to ship affordability, then shipping becomes a challenge—and if you can't ship it, it's going to be really difficult to sell online.

> **NOTE** Items that are too big to efficiently ship can be sold locally via Craigslist—although Craigslist isn't necessarily known for its crafts sales. (Learn more about selling on Craigslist in Chapter 5.)

For example, if you make handcrafted clothing, like the item in Figure 1.4, that's easy to pack and ship—perfect for online selling. On the other hand, if you sculpt big, heavy pieces out of scrap metal, the kinds of things you see displayed in public gardens, then selling online is problematic, if only because it's difficult to pack and ship these items in a cost-effective manner.

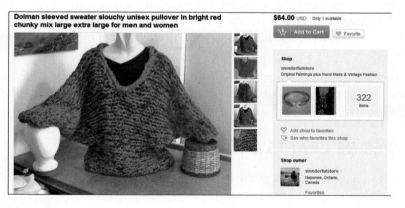

FIGURE 1.4
Handmade clothing items are easy to ship and sell online.

In other words, small and lightweight items—jewelry, ceramics, candles, paper goods, and so forth—are easily sold and shipped online. Big and heavy items—furniture, metal works, and the like—are more difficult to ship, and thus could be difficult to sell online.

> **NOTE** Learn more about shipping different types of crafts in Chapter 10, "Shipping Your Merchandise."

You also need to take fragility and perishability into account—although both are issues that can be overcome with a little work and clever thinking. A fragile glass or ceramic item, for example, can be packed in such a way to minimize potential shipping damage; it's just a matter of researching and finding the most protective packaging options. And perishable food items and plants can be shipped overnight (or, in the case of food, with dry ice) to get there plenty fresh. Do the homework, and you can find a way to ship almost anything safely and securely.

CAUTION Many sellers shy away from selling items that are easily broken during shipment. While you can improve the packaging to reduce the chance of shipping damage, you can't completely ensure safe passage. If an item does get damaged in shipment, you'll be expected to send out a replacement, at your expense, or issue a refund. That's why it's easier, especially for new sellers, to shy away from selling fragile crafts online.

There may also be legal issues with selling certain types of items online. I'd think twice, for example, before selling firearms, live animals, and even alcoholic beverages over the Internet. Not that it can't be done (many do it), it's just that there may be legal issues (some local) to deal with. Again, if you have a questionable item you want to sell, do your homework beforehand.

As you can see, then, there aren't a whole lot of restrictions as to what kinds of crafts you can and can't sell online. If in doubt, do a little Googling or search the Etsy site; if someone else is selling that kind of item, you can too.

WHAT TYPES OF CRAFTS *DO* SELL WELL ONLINE?

Now that you have some idea of the (few) types of crafts that are difficult to sell online, what categories do sell well over the Internet?

That, my friends, is a loaded question. The crafts market is constantly changing; what's hot today might be ice cold tomorrow, and tomorrow's hot item might not even exist today. That said, there are some perennially solid categories, and some types of crafts that always seem to underperform.

TIP When you're deciding what types of items to offer online, more is better. That is, you're likely to generate more sales by offering a larger selection of items. When customers have a lot of items to choose from when they're browsing your shop or site, they're more likely to purchase something than if you offer a more limited selection. It's that simple: the more you have to offer, the more potential sales you'll make.

With that in mind, here's a short list of some of the best-selling craft categories online, in alphabetical order:

- Art (paintings, photographs, prints, and so on)
- Baby items (clothing, toys, and accessories)
- Bath and body products
- Candles
- Clothing
- Jewelry
- Paper goods

> **TIP** Gift items in general sell well online. That means any craft that can be purchased and given as a gift, whether that be handmade clothing, jewelry, or whatever.

You can also go beyond traditional craft categories when selling online. For example, homemade food items sell well on Etsy, so if you're a baker or canner as well as a crafter, that's something to consider. Also worth considering are recipes and clothing patterns, both of which can be delivered electronically via email or instant download; the instant gratification of a downloadable item appeals to many buyers.

> **CAUTION** While Etsy encourages sales of edibles, it warns sellers to abide by the appropriate local laws and regulations regarding food sales. Some states, for example, require that any food packaged for resale be prepared in a commercial kitchen. Know what's acceptable in your locale before selling your edibles online.

Now, this doesn't mean that these are the only craft categories you should consider; you can generate decent sales in lots of other categories. In fact, you may find less competition in some of the lesser categories, which might be a good thing. For that matter, you might find there are too many sellers in some of the hottest categories, which can make it harder for a new seller to break in. So use this information for guidance only.

> **TIP** When selling online, price definitely matters. Many of the best-selling items on Etsy and similar sites are those crafts with lower price tags. It's the same as you experience when selling at craft shows; you'll sell more of a lower-priced item than you will of a higher-priced one. That's not to say you should sell only cheap stuff in your store, however, because quality goods always do well. Just remember to consider the price when determining what to sell.

WHY PLANNING IS A GOOD IDEA

Whatever types of crafts you offer, selling successfully is a matter of planning. The better you plan, the more successful you'll be; there are few folks who stumble into financial success.

WHAT A BUSINESS PLAN DOES FOR YOU

What this means is you need to plan for your craft-selling business. I'm talking about creating a real, honest-to-goodness business plan here, something that lays out what you want to do and how you want to do it. Think of it as a guideline or roadmap to your online selling activities, something that tells you step-by-step what you need to do to be successful. If you have a roadmap, it's relatively easy to get from point A to point B, even if you have to take a few detours here and there. Without a roadmap, you're traveling with no direction; you don't know where you're going or how to get there, so who knows where you'll end up.

If you want to be successful selling online, then you need to create a plan. Your plan will help you get ready for selling and manage your day-to-day selling activities. It will also help you determine whether or not you're successful—that is, whether you've accomplished the goals you set out in your plan. A good business is truly a set of step-by-step instructions for doing what you want to do.

THINGS YOU NEED TO PLAN

What sorts of things do you need to plan? There's a lot, really, even for smaller sellers:

- What types of crafts you want to make. (You probably already know this, but this could be an issue when you want to grow your business and add more items to your mix.)

- How to build your crafts. (Again, something you probably already know, but an issue when you need to ramp up production.)

- Where to get the materials you need for your crafts, and how much you have to pay for them.

- Where you want to sell your crafts, and what's involved in selling there—including what fees you have to pay.

- What kinds of payments you want to accept, and how you intend to process those payments.

- How you need to pack and ship the items you sell, and how much you'll need to pay for packing materials and shipping charges.

- How many items you think you'll sell—or how many you need to sell to hit a specific revenue number.

It all comes down to planning all the different items and activities that go into determining how much money you need to get started, how much time you need to spend working, and how much money you think you'll generate from your sales.

HOW MUCH PLANNING DO YOU NEED TO DO?

Not every crafter needs to do the same amount of planning. How much planning you need prepare depends somewhat on the type of seller you are (or intend to be) and what you want to get out of the experience. It takes less planning to sell the occasional item than it does to run a full-time crafts business.

THE OCCASIONAL SELLER

Many artisans create crafts in their spare time. If you have a full-time job (even if it's "just" as a housewife or mother!), craftwork can be a relaxing and fulfilling hobby that brings in a few extra dollars. You don't rely on your craft to pay the bills, but it's nice to sell something from time to time.

If this describes the way you work, you don't need to do as much upfront work as do more dedicated sellers. After all, you're not running a business here; you're engaging in a hobby that hopefully will generate a little spare income down the pike.

To that end, you probably don't need to create the same type of detailed business plan as would a larger seller. You do, however, need to work out a few details in advance, most of which having to do with money—where you want to sell, the fees involved in selling there, the materials costs to create your crafts, and the costs of packing materials and shipping. In other words, you need to know how much money you'll make from your individual craft sales; if you don't do this basic planning, you might find yourself losing money on each item you sell.

> **TIP** Key to this upfront planning is figuring out in advance how exactly you plan to ship your items, and what you need to do that—in terms of both time and materials.

You'll also want to factor in the time and expense of shooting photographs of your items, and the effort involved in creating product listings for what you're selling. If you sell unique items—that is, each item you sell is different from the last—that may be a lot of photography. If you create crafts that are essentially the same from batch to batch, you may be able to get away with a single initial photography session and then reuse those photos in future listings.

One thing you probably don't need to worry about planning is payment processing—that is, how you collect money from your buyers. If you're using eBay or Etsy or a similar site, they offer payment processing solutions (such as PayPal) that are easy to set up and use. There's not much effort required on your part.

THE GROWING SELLER

As your sales grow, your operation becomes more complex. It's good to plan for this growth, so that you're not taken unawares.

A growing seller is one who's progressed from listing a few items and registering sales when they happen to one that generates a steady stream of regular sales. It's more than making an item and then selling it (or not); it's making lots of things and expecting to sell them on a consistent basis.

When your sales start to grow, you need to plan for the extra effort. That means buying more raw materials, making more items, shooting more photos, creating more item listings, buying more packing materials, doing more packing, and making more trips to the post office. Now, you'll be compensated for this extra work (in the form of increased sales), but the work will be there, nonetheless.

You'll also have to lay out more money in advance, in the form of all those materials and supplies you'll need to purchase. That complicates planning somewhat, as you're now doing financial planning and inventory management, at least on a smallish scale.

This growth can be made easier by planning for it in advance. When you're ready to make the next steps, create a short business plan that helps you get from level A to level B. This business plan should lay out the steps you need to take to handle the growth, as well as set expectations for what you hope to sell. In other words, you're planning for the next stage, not just waiting for it to happen.

THE FULL-TIME SELLER

Then there are those who want to make a full-time business out of their craft. It's not just a matter of generating a little extra cash; it's a matter of using craft sales to pay your bills.

If you want to make online craft selling a full-time business, you need to put full-time effort into it. Running your business isn't for the lazy or faint of heart; it takes a lot of work to make a lot of individual sales. You'll spend a lot of time buying supplies, making your crafts, managing your listings, and packing and shipping your items.

When you want to turn your hobby into a business, you definitely need to plan for it. That means creating a more detailed business plan, one that outlines what you need to do, when, and how. This business plan is your own personal roadmap, as well as a budget for your business' financial needs. In fact, if you're thinking big enough, you may need to consider some sort of small business loan or line of credit to handle all the upfront expenditures you'll need to make.

CAUTION When it comes to setting up a new business, you have to spend money before you make money—your initial investment in inventory and promotion comes before you generate a single penny in sales.

In short, the bigger you want your craft selling to be, the more you need to plan for it.

PUTTING TOGETHER A NO-FRILLS BUSINESS PLAN

I hope I've convinced you of the value of planning for your online craft sales. The best way to do this is to put together a formal business plan.

Now, this doesn't have to be overly fancy nor take up a lot of time. In fact, the most useful business plans are those that flow organically from your thinking about your future business.

BEFORE YOU PLAN: THINK THINGS THROUGH

Some people start selling online without a lot of thought about it. These folks typically don't do that well; oh, some may stumble into moderate success, but most are quickly disappointed by the work involved and the results they get.

As with most things in life, there is value in thinking things through before you dive head-first into a new endeavor such as selling your crafts online. Spend a little time thinking about what you want to accomplish and how you want to accomplish it, and you'll have fewer unwelcome surprises.

What sorts of things should you be thinking about? Here's a short list to start:

- What do you like best about creating crafts? What do you like least?
- Why do you want to sell your crafts? Why do you want to sell your crafts online?
- Do you like working on your own? How much interaction with others do you want or need in the course of a day?

TIP Online selling, like craft work, is a somewhat solitary experience. If you don't like working by yourself, you might not like online selling.

- How much time can you put into both making and selling your crafts? If sales pick up, do you have extra time to spend?
- What experience do you have selling your crafts?

TIP Selling at craft shows and such is good experience for selling online. So is selling other items online, such as via eBay.

- Who are you selling to? What kind of person buys your crafts, and where do they buy them?
- What other crafters are selling your types of items online? Where are they selling? How much do their items cost?
- How much money do you have on hand, or can you round up?

TIP It takes money to buy materials and supplies; you have to spend money to make money. If you don't have enough cash on hand, you may need to borrow it—or max out your credit cards.

- How much do you really know about running a business? If you're not experienced, do you know someone who can help you with the business details—including accounting and finances?

- How much money do you want to generate from your craft sales? What level would constitute a success, and what would constitute a failure?

- How much time will you give your new business to be successful? Do you have the patience to wait several months—or longer—to become profitable?

Once you've thought about these issues—and come up with the answers—then it's time to start putting your plans on paper—in the form of a formal business plan.

PARTS OF A SUCCESSFUL BUSINESS PLAN

A business plan is just that—a plan for what you want to do with your business. It should walk you through all the steps you need to take to accomplish the goals you set.

Now, a formal business plan for a big business can be long and detailed. The business plan for your crafts business doesn't have to be either; it only has to lay out what you hope to accomplish and how you hope to accomplish it.

As such, I recommend thinking about your plan in seven parts, as follows:

NOTE This is a different and somewhat simplified structure compared to what I typically recommend for larger businesses. A more common big-company business plan consists of the following sections: Executive Summary, Vision, Mission, Opportunity, Market Strategy, Business Strategy, Organization and Operations, Management, Core Competencies and Challenges, and Financials.

- **Mission.** This is a one-sentence statement of what you intend to accomplish with your online craft selling, along the lines of "I intend to generate a part-time income selling my crafts online."

- **Market Analysis.** Before you decide how and for how much you should sell your crafts, you need to do a little market research and see how similar crafts are selling, and for how much. That means scouring Etsy and eBay and other sites for anything that somewhat resembles the crafts you create, noting prices and (if you can) sales. The information you find will help determine how to price your items and give you some sort of indication about how much you might expect to sell.

- **Product Strategy.** This could be simple—a brief description of the kinds of crafts you intend to create. You can elaborate on the obvious, however, by detailing your product costs and the creation process itself.

- **Channel Strategy.** This is where you lay out how and where you intend to sell your crafts online—which shopping sites and auctions sites and such. You should also note the fees or costs associated with each of these sales channels.

- **Promotion Strategy.** How do you intend to inform potential customers about what you have to sell? If you're on Etsy, eBay, or a similar marketplace site, the site itself is your promotion, and you may not need to do much more than create your item listings. If you run your own website, however, you will have to promote to attract traffic—and a little promotion can also help to drive your Etsy and eBay traffic, too. Consider how you'll use Pinterest and similar social media, how you'll optimize your website and listings for search engines, and whether you need to advertise—and if so, how much.

- **Goals.** This is where you lay out just how many sales you hope or expect to make, and from there calculate how much profit you'll generate. Yes, that means projecting sales numbers as well as working through all your expenses, both fixed and on a per-item basis. This needn't be too complex; it's easy enough to calculate how much it costs to make each item, and then to tally all your fixed expenses—your labor, utilities, website hosting fees, and so forth. A little back-of-the-envelope math may be good enough, especially if you're an occasional or growing seller. For larger sellers, you'll probably want to hire an accountant at some point.

- **Risks.** Let's finish your business plan by being realistic about things—in particular, those things that can go wrong. Maybe you won't sell as much as you thought, or maybe your materials could become more expensive, or maybe you won't have enough free time to keep up with demand. In any instance, forewarned is forearmed; be honest about the risks you face, just in case.

And that's your plan. You start by stating what you intend to do, you take a look at what others are doing, you figure out how to make your crafts, you determine how you'll sell them and promote them, you set forth your goals and calculate how much money you'll make if you achieve them, and then you evaluate the obstacles you might face in getting everything done. It's terrific preparation for getting your sales off the ground—and a surprisingly easy-to-follow set of instructions for doing what you hope to do.

TALKING THROUGH YOUR PLAN

Working through a seven-part business plan might seem daunting. But it needn't be. In fact, I think it's a fairly easy thing to do, if you approach it properly.

To me, the best way to get cracking on a business plan is to think of it like a conversation with a friend, over coffee or a beer or whatever your beverage of choice may be. Sit down for a ten-minute conversation and tell your friend about what you hope to do with your craft business, and you have the bones of your business plan.

Let me explain.

Telling a friend about your craft-selling plans walks you through the exact same steps you need to create your business plan. Assuming that you're somewhat enthusiastic about what you plan to do, this shouldn't be a difficult task.

Let's do an example. Imagine that you create gift baskets and are sitting down with a friend to tell her what you're up to. The conversation might go something like this:

"Let me tell you about what I plan to do. I make gift baskets, and want to sell them online. They're very popular with women, especially older women, who buy them for gifts.

"I did a search on Etsy and found that the average gift basket sells for about $50, and as near as I can tell, in an average week it looks as if it's a pretty popular category. I think my gift baskets are better quality than the ones I see from other sellers, so I should be able to compete with what's currently available.

"I've been doing this for a while, and I know I can make at least one gift basket a day, in the evenings, after dinner. "It costs me about $5 in materials to make each basket, and if I value my labor at $10 an hour, that's about $25 to make each basket.

"I want to get started by selling on Etsy, which is a good site for these kinds of crafts. I'll open up an Etsy shop and list a half-dozen different types of gift baskets, to begin with. Each listing costs $0.20 apiece, so I have to add that to my costs. I'll also have to figure in Etsy's 3.5% transaction fee, or $1.75 per basket sold. There's also a 3% payment processing fee, plus a flat $0.25 for each transaction, so there's another $1.75 in costs. When I add all of Etsy's fees to my materials and labor costs, I'm up to $28.50 per basket sold. That's still a good profit for a $50 sale.

"Since Etsy drives a lot of craft-buying traffic, I don't think I need to do any additional advertising for my crafts. I will post my baskets to Pinterest, which will provide some additional exposure at no extra cost.

"Based on what I see other sellers doing, I expect to sell two or three items a week. If it's just two baskets a week, that's $100 in sales or $45 in profit. Over the course of a year, that's $5,200 in sales, or $2,340 in profit. Not bad for a little after dinner work.

"Now, I could be wrong and only sell half that much. If that's the case, that's still an extra $20 a week or so in my pocket, and that's okay. And if sales really take off, I can work a little harder on weekends and make up to ten baskets a week, which I wouldn't mind doing. So I'm okay if things go really well or not well at all."

As you can see, this short story (a little over 400 words) tells your friend everything she needs to know about your planned business. It also tells you everything you need to complete your business plan. All you have to do is put your conversation down on paper.

WRITING THE PLAN

Which brings us to the process of writing your business plan. I can already hear you sighing; that's a lot of work, I know. But it really isn't. You don't have to be a great writer to create a workable business plan.

All you have to do is write seven paragraphs, each no more than a few sentences long. If you can, just write down what you said (or would say) in that conversation with a friend. You can write it down verbatim, in sentence format, or in abbreviated, bullet-point format. That's right, a decent business plan can be written as all short bullets.

The goal, after all, isn't to convince a banker or group of investors to lend you thousands of dollars. The goal is to help you get started, and to help you measure your success at some point down the line. Write down just enough detail to guide the way, and you've done a good job.

YOU'VE PLANNED THE PLAN: NOW WHAT?

As I've said, a business plan is a set of instructions for what you intend to do. What, then, do you generally do with a set of instructions? Follow them!

That's right, the first thing you do with your business plan is follow it. You wrote down what you expect to do, so get cracking and do it. Follow the steps in your plan and start selling online. Now.

Once you get started, you can go back to your plan to see how your actual sales are matching up with your expectations. Wait a few months—three, maybe six—and then compare your actual sales to what you'd planned. Are you selling as many items as you'd hoped? If so, great! If not, why not?

Or maybe sales are greater than you hoped. If so, what are you doing right? More important, how are you handling the extra work?

And don't just look at sales; also look at your costs, and the time expended. Are your actual costs in line with your planned ones? If not, what can you do to reduce costs—or increase your selling prices? Are you making a profit on your sales? Enough of one? Is the return worth the work you're putting into it?

Once you've evaluated your performance, go back and revise your plan for the next six months or a year. If sales are lower than expected, plan for that; if they're higher, plan for more growth. A business plan is a living document that changes based on what happens in the real world. It gets you started and helps keep you on track—which is why it's worth doing, even if you're just an occasional seller.

Setting the Right Price

2

Whatever type of craft you want to sell online, you have to determine the right selling price. Price your item too high and nobody will buy it; price it too low and you might not make any profit.

As you can imagine, setting prices is as much an art as it is a science—which should be right up the alley for all you serious artisans!

RESEARCHING THE MARKET

Before we start calculating costs and profit margins and the like, it helps to know what price others are selling similar crafts for. While you shouldn't set your price solely based on what other sellers are doing, you also don't want to price your items too much above or below the going price of similar items. Set your price too high (no matter how much better quality you offer) and people will skip your items in favor of lower-priced alternatives; set your price too low and you'll be passing up profits.

What you need to do, then, is research the market. Go to Etsy and eBay and similar sites and search for the types of crafts you'll be selling. Look at the prices of items available for sale, of course, but also the prices of items that actually sold. Try to get a feel for the average selling price, or at least a common price range. You can then use this data to inform your own pricing decision.

CAUTION   Just because a seller is asking a certain price doesn't mean that the item will actually sell at that price. There are a lot of overpriced crafts online that don't sell at all.

You can also use this type of market research to determine how popular a given type of craft or category is. For example, if you sell handmade candles, you may find there are lots of them offered for sale online, in a variety of fragrances. While vanilla candles might be very popular, there may be so many other crafters selling them that you'd do better offering a different scent.

Where do you do this type of research? The most obvious approach is to simply browse or search the craft listings at the top craft-related websites—Etsy, eBay, and the like. There are also a few research-specific sites that consolidate sales data from other sites that can make your research easier.

For example, I like to peruse the data assembled at the Craft Count site (www.craftcount.com). As you can see in Figure 2.1, Craft Count tracks sales on the Etsy site; you can browse the top sellers overall (and then see what types of items they sell), as well as the top sellers by category.

If you want to research craft sales on eBay, there are a few different tools available—none of them free, unfortunately. For example, HammerTap (www.hammertap.com) provides information about sell-through rates, selling prices, and effective keywords, for $7.99/month. The competing Terapeak (www.terapeak.com) runs $29.95/month, but offers more detailed sales data by category or for specific products.

FIGURE 2.1
Researching top Etsy sellers by category on the Craft Count website.

> ✂ **TIP** Since eBay research tools are so expensive, you may want to subscribe for a month or so when you're just starting out, and then cancel your subscription. Even better, both HammerTap and Terapeak offer free trials you can take advantage of.

Whichever research tool you use, the point is to get out there and see what's going on before you decide what to sell and for how much. Don't start selling online with your eyes closed; see what others are doing and how successful they are at it. It'll help you make smarter decisions.

CALCULATING YOUR COSTS

Of course, before you set your final selling price, you need to determine the actual cost of the item. I'm not talking just the cost of those materials you used to make the item; an item's total cost includes both the cost of materials and the cost of the labor it took to make it. (For most crafters, that's *your* labor, by the way.)

You can get pretty fancy when calculating item costs, but the following simple formula tends to work more often than not:

Item cost = cost of materials + cost of labor

Let's look at what this means.

CALCULATING MATERIALS COSTS

The cost of materials is simple; that's whatever you paid for the materials required to make the item. This is a variable cost, in that you only pay it when you make an item. If you make handmade quilts, for example, your cost of materials is the cloth and thread used to make each quilt; if you make bead bracelets, your cost of materials are the beads and thread.

> **NOTE** In accounting terms, your materials cost is called the *cost of goods sold*.

Now, calculating your materials cost may not be so straightforward. Take the quilt example, where you probably buy your raw materials in bulk. You might purchase $500 in quilt squares at a time, but only use a quarter of them for each quilt. That means your cost of materials for each individual quilt is 1/4 times the $500 bulk expenditure, or $125. You still spent the whole $500, of course, but you can only assign a quarter of that expenditure to each individual quilt.

CALCULATING LABOR COSTS

The cost of labor is a bit more difficult to calculate; it's really how much you'd pay someone (or pay yourself) to make that item. If you actually do pay someone else to make the item, this expense is easy to figure, because you know the amount paid. If you make the item yourself, however, you have to set a rate for your own labor.

Just what is your time worth? If you pay yourself minimum wage ($7.25 in most states) and spend two hours assembling an item, that's a cost of labor of $14.50. I'm guessing, however, that you value your work at more than minimum wage, which means you have to set a fair wage for what you personally do. Is your time worth $10 an hour? $15? $20? You decide, then calculate that rate times the number of hours it takes to make an item.

> **NOTE** Note that we haven't yet discussed *fixed costs*—rent, telephone, website hosting, and the like, or what some call *overhead*. That's because you typically don't figure fixed costs into the item pricing equation. Instead, your fixed costs are paid for out of your per-item gross profits. That is, if an item cost you $10 to make and $25 to sell, you make a gross profit of $15 per item. That $15 gross profit goes toward paying your fixed costs. (And hopefully you generate enough profit to cover all those fixed costs!)

CALCULATING SELLING FEES

When you're selling online, there's one more category of variable costs to add to the equation—your selling fees. These are the per-transaction fees you pay to the selling site. Sites such as Etsy and eBay typically charge a fixed fee for each item you list for sale, as well as a percentage of the final selling price when you actually sell an item. You'll also pay a percentage to the site or a third-party service (such as PayPal) for payment processing. These fees need to be added to your cost equation, as follows:

Item cost = cost of materials + cost of labor + listing fees + selling fees + payment processing fees

These fees differ from site to site, of course, so you'll want to determine how much you'll owe before you create a listing. You can then include those costs in your item cost calculations.

CALCULATING PACKAGING COSTS

But wait—there's more! When you're selling online, you have to consider the variable cost of *packaging*. Not shipping, because you pass that along to the buyer. I'm talking the cost of the box or envelope you use to ship each item you sell, as well as all related packing materials—Styrofoam peanuts, bubble wrap, you name it. This means you need to figure out how you're packing each item in advance, but that's just part of your normal pre-selling homework. Given the challenges in packing large, fragile, or perishable items, the cost of packaging can be significant. So figure it out and add it to our formula, as follows:

Item cost = cost of materials + cost of labor + listing fees + selling fees + payment processing fees + cost of packaging

And that should do it.

CALCULATING THE SELLING PRICE

Okay, now that you know how much it costs to make an item, and what similar items are selling for online, it's time to set your pricing. Again, we can get pretty fancy about how we do this, but for most crafters, the following simple formula will get you in the ball-park:

Selling price = item cost x 4

Simple, huh? Just take all your variable costs—materials, labor, selling fees, and packaging—and multiply that number by four. So, for example, if your item costs total $10 for an item, you should sell it online for $40.

WHY 4 X COSTS WORKS

Does that sound excessive to you? It shouldn't, for a couple of reasons.

First, you have to make a profit to cover all your fixed costs that we have yet accounted for. Rent, equipment, and the like adds up fast, and if you don't make enough gross profit, you can't cover your overhead.

Second, you need to leave yourself some wiggle room to discount the items you sell. A serious craft seller will occasionally need to promote her items—maybe offer a 20% discount for a limited time, or do a buy one get one free deal, or whatever it takes to spice things up for buyers. (Figure 2.2 shows a discounted listing on the Etsy site.) If you set your selling price too low, there's not enough profit in the mix to allow for this sort of discounting.

FIGURE 2.2

Set your initial price high enough that you can discount your item if necessary—and still make a profit.

Let me show you what I mean. Let's say you have $10 in fixed costs and price your item at $40, leaving a $30 gross profit. If you decide to run a sale offering all your items for 40% off, that means you'd sell your $40 item for $24. (The 40% discount figures to $16 off your normal price.) That leaves you a $14 gross profit on the item, which is still livable. If, on the other hand, you'd only priced your item at $20 to begin with (figuring that a $10 profit was enough), when you go 40% off, you'll be selling your item for $12—and that meager $2 profit won't pay for a lot of overhead.

> ✂ **TIP** You can list sales and discounts directly on the Etsy site, or through third-party sites such as Etsy on Sale (www.etsyonsale.com).

FINE-TUNING YOUR SELLING PRICE

Don't take this simple formula as a hard and fast rule, however. While this calculation will get you in the ballpark, price-wise, you may still need to fine-tune the final price in a number of ways.

First, if you follow the "4 x" rule precisely, you'll probably end up with a price that isn't a price—that is, one that ends in odd numbers. Since most selling prices end in even numbers, or in "9," this could be offputting to potential customers.

For example, if your costs total $7.86 and you multiply that number by 4, you end up with the unappealing selling price of $31.44. Have you ever seen an item in store or at a craft fair priced at $31.44? Of course not—which means you either want to round down to $30 (or $29.99) or round up to $32 or so. It's an aesthetic thing, but it makes a difference. (Figure 2.3 shows pricing within a specific Etsy category—everything ends in an even number.)

Second, and more important, your calculated price may not be in line with the average selling price of similar items from other crafters. This is why you do your market research up front, to determine the typical price range for your type of craft. Just because your calculations put you at a specific price, you may discover that this price is too high or too low, compared to what else is out there.

Let's say you have an item with $10 in costs which, using the "4 x" calculation, you'd price at $40. Fine and dandy, but what if you do your research and determine that most similar items are selling in the $35 range? You could stick to your guns and keep your price at $40, but you probably wouldn't make a lot of sales. The better response might be to lower your price to $35, which still gives you a decent $25 profit per item and will likely generate more sales.

FIGURE 2.3

Pricing on the Etsy site—no odd numbers here.

What if you discover your price is too low? While it's nice to be the most competitive player in the market, you may be leaving money on the table. Take our $10 cost/$40 price example again, but this time you discover similar crafts are selling for $50 on Etsy and other sites. Well, you could leave your price at $40 and undercut the competition, but pricing at $50 would still be competitive and bring in $10 more per sale. Or you could split the difference and price your item at $45—still five bucks less than the competition, but putting five additional dollars of profit in your pocket.

> **TIP**   You'll also want to fine-tune your price over time, based on your own selling experience. If you find that sales are slow, you might want to lower your price a bit. If sales are robust, maybe you can enact a slight price increase to improve your profitability. Price doesn't have to remain constant over time; adjusting up or down based on actual sales makes a lot of sense.

The key, then, is to combine your cost analysis/pricing calculation with knowledge you glean from market research. You can fine-tune your pricing up or down as necessary to both be competitive and profitable.

> ✂ **TIP** You have to get the price right, but price isn't the only thing customers care about. Yes, some folks buy purely on price—which is especially true for commodity products. But craft buyers are buying something unique from a talented artisan, and price is only part of the equation; they're interested in style and appearance and whether or not they like an item. They also care about the seller, and the image you project. In many instances, customers will pay more for a quality item, a unique item, or an item from a trusted seller.

CALCULATING PROFIT

So far we've focused on costs and selling price. But those two factors work together to give your profit, which is the actual cash you get to put into your pocket at the end of the day. Profits are what's really important.

UNDERSTANDING GROSS AND NET

Some accounting basics first. There are two types of profits—gross profits and net profits. You need to know the difference between the two, as follows:

- **Gross profit** is the difference between your selling price and your item costs, on an individual item basis. If you sell an item for $30 and it costs you $10, you make a gross profit of $20 on that item. (That's $30 minus $10.)
- **Net profit** is the difference between your total gross profit and your fixed expenses for your entire business. For example, if you generate $500 in net profit for the month but have $400 in fixed expenses (telephone, advertising, rent, whatever), you make a net profit of $100 for that month.

Or, put in formulaic form:

Gross profit = Selling price – item cost

Net profit = Gross profit – fixed expenses

In other words, gross profit is how you measure the profitability of any given item or sale. Net profit is how you measure the profitability of the total sales of your business.

ARE YOU MAKING MONEY?

Which is more important? Well, for each item you sell, you have to focus on its own gross profit. But for your entire business—all your selling activities—it's net profit that literally pays the bills.

What do you do when you calculate your profit—gross or net—and discover that it's negative? That means you're not making a profit; you're generating a loss. This is not a good thing, and you need to address it. (Assuming, that is, you don't like losing money on your craft selling.)

> **NOTE**   Learn more about gross and net profit (and other accounting stuff) in Chapter 15, "Measuring Your Success."

CONSIDERING WHOLESALE PRICING

So far in this chapter, we've talked exclusively about retail sales and your crafts' retail price. If, at some point in time, you have the opportunity to sell your crafts to other sellers, you'll need to set a significantly lower *wholesale price* to offer to these resellers. That is, the other sellers will buy your goods from you at the wholesale price, and then sell them to their customers at the retail price.

> **NOTE**   The retail selling price is sometimes called suggested retail price or list price.

This means, of course, that the wholesale price you offer resellers must be significantly less than the retail price at which you sell to your regular customers. A good rule of thumb is that resellers purchase items at 50% off the normal retail price, so that they can make a decent profit margin. So you can calculate your whole sale price like this:

Wholesale price = Retail price x 50%

Or, looking at it from the ground up, you can calculate wholesale price based on your item costs:

Wholesale price = Item cost x 2

So your wholesale price is 2 x your item cost, and your retail price is 2 x your wholesale price. As an example, if you have an item with a $10 cost, you sell it wholesale at $20 or at retail for $40.

> **TIP**   You make less money on each wholesale sale, but make it up in volume. (Presumably, anyway.) The whole point of selling to other resellers is that they'll buy multiple quantities, not one at a time. It's a great way to increase your sales (and profits) if you can find an online or offline store interested in reselling your crafts.

Putting Together a Successful Listing

3

When you have a craft to sell online, you need to tell people about it. No matter how you choose to sell your crafts—which site or sites you use—you need to write a compelling description of what you're selling. That includes a captivating title and fully descriptive text.

This isn't just "something you have to do," either; it may be the most important part of the selling process. (After making the craft itself, of course.) It's a fact that the better written and more effective your listing title and description, the more items you'll sell. It's just like advertising copy or product copy in a catalog: Great copy produces the best results.

WRITING AN ATTENTION-GRABBING TITLE

Let's start right at the top, with the title of your item listing. This is the first thing most potential customers see—and if it isn't compelling, the *only* thing.

Figure 3.1 shows a typical Etsy listing. The title appears at the top of the listing, in larger bold type; your eye is drawn to the title as well as to the image of the product.

Figure 3.2 shows a similar listing on the eBay site. The title is also prominent here, even though it's scooted to the right a bit. Again, it's one of the first and most important things a shopper sees.

FIGURE 3.1
A typical Etsy listing, with prominent bold title.

FIGURE 3.2
An equally bold title in an eBay craft listing.

With this in mind, you need to accomplish two things with your listing title:

- Make sure your title is included in the search results when someone is searching for your type of item.

- Include the appropriate information so that anyone searching for a similar craft will find your item in his or her search results.

How well you do both will determine how well your item sells.

CREATING A SEARCHABLE TITLE

Let's tackle the first point first. Most customers find the items they want by using a given site's search feature, or by searching Google for a site selling that craft. That means your title needs to be written in a way that it gets noticed by a site's search engine.

Now, search results pages differ from site to site; some show only the title, others show the title and a small thumbnail, while still others show a larger thumbnail along with the title. For example, eBay's search results pages, shown in Figure 3.3, display the full item title and a small thumbnail picture. Etsy's search results, in contrast, display a much larger image but only the first 24 characters or so of the title, as you can see in Figure 3.4.

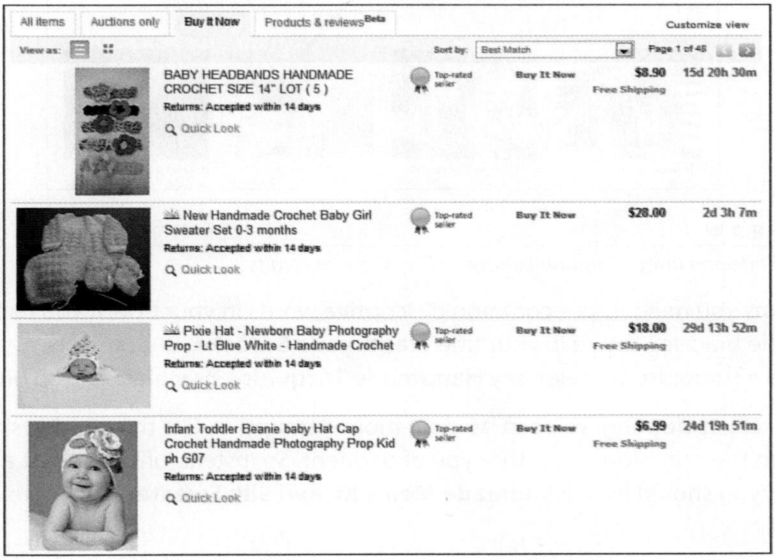

FIGURE 3.3

Full title and small thumbnail image in eBay's search results.

Whichever selling site you use, you need to construct your title so that it includes the words that people will be searching for—what webbie types call *keywords*. If your title includes the right keywords, it will be a match for more searchers; screw up the keywords, and your crafts will not show up in customers' search results.

To make sure your title matches the most possible queries, you have to think like the people who will be looking for your crafts. Use the words that they are likely to use. Include the name of the item—both the "official" name and any more common name it might have. Include the color, the size, and the materials used. Include whatever terms you typically use to describe the item. The more search words you can include, the better.

FIGURE 3.4
Partial title and large thumbnail image in Etsy's search results.

This means you need to use common descriptive words in your title. If you're selling a handmade bracelet, say so in your title: **Handmade Bracelet**. But be more descriptive, if you can. If it's a turquoise bracelet, say **Handmade Turquoise Bracelet**. And so on.

If you're selling clothing, you can be even more descriptive. Get the gender, size, color, and fabric into the title, along with the type of garment. So instead of selling just a **Handmade Sweater**, you should list a **Handmade Men's XL Red Silk Sweater**. The more descriptive, the better.

Once again, it's important to think how people are going to search, and then tailor your title appropriately.

> ✂ **TIP**   It's a good idea to enter the singular form of words into your title, rather than the plural form. When you use the singular, your item should come up as a hit for both singular- and plural-form searches; if you enter the plural form, you may be excluded from singular-form searches. For example, if your title is **Vanilla Candle**, it will match searches for both **candle** and **candles**. If your title is **Vanilla Candles**, it may be excluded from the results when someone searches for **candle**, singular.

MAKING YOUR TITLE POP

Beyond including as many relevant facts as possible in your title, how do you make your title POP off the page and STAND OUT from all the other boring listings? Obviously, one technique is to employ the judicious use of CAPITAL LETTERS. The operative word here is *judicious*; titles with ALL capital letters step over the line into overkill.

Thinking like an advertising copywriter also pays off. What words almost always stop consumers in their tracks? Use attention-getting words such as **FREE** and **NEW** and **BONUS** and **EXTRA** and **DELUXE** and **RARE**—as long as these words truly describe the item you're selling and don't mislead potential customers. (And don't bump more important search words for these fluffier marketing terms—that won't help your item show up in search results.)

CAUTION Don't go overboard on non-descriptive title words. In particular, you should avoid unnecessary use of special characters (#, *, !, and the like); they're the equivalent of wasted calories, in that they don't help you in the search results.

In short, use your title to both inform and attract attention—and include as many potential search keywords as possible.

WATCH THE LENGTH

Most sites limit the length of your title, in terms of number of characters, so you have to be both effective and efficient. For example, Etsy limits your titles to 155 characters; eBay has an even stricter 80-character title limit. That means you need to be efficient in your titling—which sometimes requires a bit of creativity.

One way to save on title length is to use common abbreviations that anyone shopping for a certain type of craft will know, even if they're little-used by the more general public. For example, the abbreviation OOAK stands for One Of a Kind, and takes up a lot less space in a listing's title than spelling it all out.

TIP If you use an abbreviation in the item title, you might want to spell out the entire term in the description—for the benefit of less-knowledgeable shoppers.

There are tons of these common abbreviations you can use in your listing titles. Table 3.1 lists some of the more common ones.

Table 3.1   Abbreviations and Acronyms

Abbreviation	Description
ACEO	Art Cards, Editions, and Originals
AOP	Artist's Own Pattern
BFSC	Built From Scratch Clothing
BOGO	Buy One, Get One (Free)
COA	Certificate of Authenticity
HTF	Hard to Find
OOAK	One Of a Kind
OSWOA	Original Small Work of Art
SRA	Self-Representing Artist
SRAJD	Self-Representing Artist Jewelry Designer

Naturally, specific types of crafts will have their own acronyms and abbreviations, and you should use them when appropriate. The point is to conserve title words for those words most meaningful to potential buyers; when you can abbreviate something, do it.

CREATING A DESCRIPTIVE DESCRIPTION

If the title is the headline of your item listing, the description is your listing's body copy. This means it's time to put on your copywriter's hat and get down to the nitty-gritty details.

What makes for a great listing description? Remember, you have all the space you need (there's no practical character limit, as there is with the item title), so say as much as you need to say. You don't have to scrimp on words or leave anything out. If you can describe your craft adequately in a sentence, great; if it takes three paragraphs, that's okay, too. (Just make sure you break your info into easily digestible chunks; three short paragraphs is better than one overly long one!)

Figure 3.5 shows a typical item description on the Etsy site. Note how the listing includes all the relevant details, presented in multiple short paragraphs. It's easy to read and gives shoppers everything they need to know about the item. Your descriptions should do the same.

FIGURE 3.5
A typical Etsy product description.

INCLUDE ALL THE DETAILS

When you're writing the description for your listing, make sure you mention anything and everything that a potential buyer might need to know. Shoppers expect to see certain key data points in your item description; they include

- **Type of craft.** What exactly is the thing you're selling? It may be obvious to you, but not necessarily to potential buyers. Go into detail—if it's a table lamp made from a bowling ball, say so.

- **Potential customers.** Who is your piece designed for? Who can best use or enjoy it?

> **TIP** If your piece is specifically *not* for a particular audience, state that, too. For example, if your item has lots of small pieces that might prove to be a choking hazard for young children, say so.

- **Function.** What does your piece do, if anything? Does it have a useful function, or is it just for decoration only?

- **Functionality.** How does your piece work? Are there buttons, or a zipper, or a clasp, or Velcro, or what? Does it need to be assembled? Does it need batteries? Let shoppers know beforehand.

- **Size.** This is especially important for clothing. Give the precise size—and if something fits a little oversized or undersized, say so.

- **Dimensions and other important measurements.** Don't just say something is "large" or "small"—give precise measurements.

- **Weight.** This is especially important if it's a heavy item; less important if your item weighs less than a few pounds.

- **Color.** Don't rely on pictures alone; describe the color as best you can in words. And don't be generic; saying something is ruby or cherry or burgundy is more useful than using the generic "red."

- **Materials or contents.** Tell potential buyers what an item is made of. That means the fabric if you're selling clothing, but also the specific materials you used when created other types of crafts. And if there's something inside your item, describe that, too.

- **Techniques.** How did you make this item? Did you knit it, sew it, weave it, or what? This helps to tell the story of your piece and gives useful information to potential buyers.

- **Feel and smell.** Provide a tactile description of your item. Is it soft or hard? Rough or smooth? Does it have a scent? Try to provide the complete in-person experience in words.

> **TIP** If you're selling edible items, describe how the item tastes.

- **Accessories.** If anything comes with the item, tell potential buyers. For example, a selection of handmade soaps might come in a gift box, or you might include some extra cloth squares with your handmade quilt.

- **Any known defects or damage.** Be honest. If an item isn't perfect, say so. It'll save you a world of trouble in the end.

- **Warranty or guarantee.** If you offer a money-back guarantee or other warranty on your items, say so. If you don't, say that all sales are final. Again, it pays to be upfront about all the details.

In other words, you need to include everything a potential buyer needs to know to make an informed buying decision. Don't leave any questions unanswered; include all the facts there are. The more descriptive you are, the more comfortable a shopper will be in purchasing your item.

> **TIP** I like the advice that you should write your description as if you had no pictures—that is, as if you're describing your item to someone over the phone. (Likewise, there's the corollary advice to take your pictures as if you had no written description, which is equally useful.)

PRIORITIZE YOUR INFORMATION

Unlike the listing title, there are few space restrictions on your item description. You don't have to scrimp on words or leave anything out, so you can say as much as you need to say. If you can describe your item adequately in a sentence, great; if it takes three paragraphs, that's okay too.

That said, not everyone will read all of a longer description. With that in mind, you need to prioritize the information you present. Put the most important information first—in the very first paragraph—since a lot of folks won't read any further than that. Think of your first paragraph like a lead paragraph in a newspaper story: Grab 'em with something catchy, give them the gist of the story, and lead them into reading the next paragraph and the one after that.

> **CAUTION** Even though you *can* write pages and pages of descriptive copy, that doesn't mean you *should*. There is much value in writing a clear and concise description. People will only read so much; don't blather on!

By the way, I really like information presented in bulleted lists. A bulleted list is much easier to scan than a long paragraph. When you can break your description into lists, do; it's a great way to present detailed information in an easily-digested fashion.

STRESS BENEFITS, NOT FEATURES

While you need to describe the unique features of what you're selling, you also need to stress the benefits of those features. That's Marketing 101—customers want to know what the product can do for them, to make their lives easier or better or more enjoyable.

Just so we're clear on what's what, a feature is something your item has; a benefit is something your item does for the buyer. So if you're selling a handmade sweater, you can mention that it has four buttons and a sophisticated pattern; those are features. But it's more important that you say it's stylish or will keep the wearer warm on cool fall nights; those are benefits. Bottom line, benefits matter more than features.

> **TIP** Always check the spelling and grammar of your item descriptions. If your copy is shoddy, customers may think your crafts are shoddy, too.

USE POWER WORDS—BUT AVOID SUPERLATIVES

As with the listing title, you can and should use power words in your item description. I'm talking words like FREE and BONUS and DELUXE and RARE—as long as these words truly describe the item you're selling and don't mislead the potential buyer.

That said, there's no need to sound like a carnival barker. State the facts, but don't exaggerate or overuse superlatives. There's no need to say that you're selling a **HUGE HUGE LOT!** Let the facts speak for themselves; don't unnecessarily pump them up.

> **CAUTION** I'd like to think that this one is obvious, but I've seen enough bad auction descriptions to know otherwise. Never, I repeat NEVER, write your description in all capital letters!

ADD YOUR PERSONAL STYLE

To create a more powerful item listing, you need to pay attention to both content and style—that is, the specific words you write and the way you present those words on the page. Do so, and you'll notice the results.

Remember that selling crafts is a more personal endeavor than selling paper clips or groceries. Each piece you create is unique, and a unique selling opportunity. The more you can personalize the selling experience, the more invested potential buyers will be.

To that end, I recommend that you talk about your crafts in the first person. It's good to tell shoppers that "I make every single medallion" or "I spent ten hours working on this quilt." That personalizes the experience and makes buyers feel like they know you.

You should also feel free to let your personality come through in your item listings. Don't be a robot, or write like one; write the same way you talk, so that shoppers fell as if you're talking directly to them. (Use correct grammar, of course; you shouldn't talk like an illiterate hick!)

I also like the concept of telling the story of the pieces you create. Tell shoppers why you made this item, what inspired you. Try to impart some of your love of the craft; tell how you made the item, any issues you ran into or interesting facts you discovered. Make it personal, and make it fun.

The point is that most craft buyers are not buying dishwater detergent, they're buying something personal. They don't want faceless, anonymous goods; they want a piece that's personal to them, that comes with a story. Take the time to tell the story of what you created, and you'll hook that craft buyer.

DON'T FORGET THE PICTURES!

Every craft listing you create should be accompanied by one or more pictures of the item you created. In the craft market, photos are every bit as important as words, if not more so. To that end, I've devoted an entire chapter to help you take the best possible photos of your crafts. Turn the page to learn more!

Taking Powerful Pictures

4

Writing an effective title and description is necessary for any craft listing on any marketplace. Equally important to the text you write are the photos you show of your craft items. People want to see an item before they buy it, which means you need product photos to successfully sell online. In fact, the better your photos, the more items you'll sell—and at higher prices, too.

Great product photos don't come from the camera in your iPhone taken with natural room light. You need to know a little bit about good photography to take appealing photos of your crafts. It also helps, of course, if you have a photo editing program to make your photos look even better—and to fix any mistakes you make.

WHAT YOU NEED TO TAKE EFFECTIVE PRODUCT PHOTOS

Taking an effective photo of a craft for an item listing takes a bit of effort; it's not quite as easy as snapping off a quick one with your cell phone camera. To take quality photos of the items you intend to sell, you'll need a decent digital camera and a variety of photographic accessories, including

- Digital camera
- Tripod
- Auxiliary lighting
- Clean space with plain black or white background
- Photo editing software

Let's take a detailed look at everything you need.

CHOOSING THE RIGHT DIGITAL CAMERA

Seems like every digital device these days has a built-in camera. Your cell phone has a camera, your iPad has a camera, even your computer comes with a little webcam device of sorts. This proliferation of picture-taking devices should make it easier to shoot photos of your craft work—right?

Wrong. The problem with still cameras embedded in other-purpose devices is that they aren't that good. Even when they up the pixel count (as is the case with the iPhone 4S, which takes 8 megapixel photos), you're still dealing with a small device with a mediocre lens—and it's the lens that makes a big difference. No multi-purpose device today has the same type of high-quality lens you find on even the lowest-price point-and-shoot digital cameras, and you can tell the difference in the resulting photos.

If you're serious about selling your crafts online, you need to take the best photos possible, and that means purchasing a dedicated digital camera. The good news is that you don't need a really high-end model. What you want to focus on is the lens quality, not the number of megapixels.

> **NOTE** In almost every case, you'll need to reduce the size of your photos from the default resolution of your camera when you upload them to your item listing. That means going with an uber-high resolution camera is wasted pixels; you can't display that many pixels on a web page.

That doesn't mean you can get by with the cheapest camera available, however. To take good product photos, you want a camera with a quality lens, preferably with at least 3X optical zoom, and with a macro mode. (You use the macro mode to take close-up photos of those very small items you have for sale.) While you can go with a more expensive digital SLR, like the one in Figure 4.1, that may be overkill; most basic point-and-shoot models do the job. (Figure 4.2 shows a basic point-and-shoot digital camera with a decent lens for shooting craft photos.)

FIGURE 4.1

Nikon's D3200 digital SLR camera—takes great pictures, but may be overkill for shooting craft photos.

FIGURE 4.2

Canon's PowerShot ELPH 310 HS point-and-shoot digital camera—an inexpensive alternative for shooting photos of your crafts.

GOING STEADY WITH A TRIPOD

When you're spending $100 or more for a decent digital camera, hold a few bucks back for those accessories that will help you take better photos every time. The most essential accessory is the humble tripod, which holds your camera steady when you're taking photos.

A good tripod, like the one in Figure 4.3, will help you avoid camera shake and corresponding blurry pictures. It's also useful in low-light situations, where you need to hold your camera especially still for long exposures. And it's not expensive; you can pick up a decent tripod for less than $50.

FIGURE 4.3

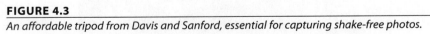

An affordable tripod from Davis and Sanford, essential for capturing shake-free photos.

ENHANCING YOUR PHOTOS WITH AUXILIARY LIGHTING

To take professional-looking product photos, you need professional-quality lighting. That means something more than natural room light, which simply isn't bright enough or diffused enough to make your crafts look their best. For that matter, the flash lighting built into most digital cameras isn't that good either, especially when you're shooting product photos; it's too direct and tends to create unwanted shadows.

What you need to do is invest in external lighting of some sort. If you have a digital SLR camera that accepts this type of accessory, you can add an external flash kit, sometimes called a *speed light*, like the one in Figure 4.4. This type of external flash has several advantages over your camera's built-in flash.

FIGURE 4.4

Use a speed light with a digital SLR camera (such as this Canon model) to provide more professional lighting.

First, a speed light has a longer throw, meaning you can get more consistent light over a longer distance. Second, the speed light's power can be dialed down, providing more subtle lighting. And third, the speed light's head can be swiveled or angled up or down, providing bounce lighting instead of direct lighting, which results in less harsh lighting effects. The result is less glare, fewer unwanted shadows, and little or no red eye when shooting people.

Even better, if slightly more expensive, is an external lighting kit. This type of kit includes two or more photo floodlights that you can position in front of, to the sides, or behind the items you photograph. (Some kits, such as the one in Figure 4.5, encase the lights in softboxes, for more diffused lighting.)

TIP While you can purchase photofloods separately, the better option for most craft sellers is to purchase a prepackaged lighting kit. These kits typically contain two or three photofloods, stands to hold the lights, and some sort of diffuser for each light. You can find two-piece lighting kits starting under $200, at your local camera supply store.

FIGURE 4.5

An external lighting kit with freestanding softboxes, from StarLite.

KEEPING IT PLAIN WITH PHOTO BACKGROUNDS

You also need to think about where you'll be taking your photos. You'll need some sort of flat surface, such as a table, to place your crafts. You'll also need some sort of simple background—black, white, or some other color that contrasts well (and doesn't detract from) the item you're shooting.

You may be able to create an effective background from an appropriate expanse of colored cardboard or cloth. More professional results, however, come from using a roll of colored background paper or cloth, which provides a seamless background. You typically hang the background between two stands, as shown in Figure 4.6, and position the item you're shooting on a table in front of it.

> **TIP** When choosing a background color, know that white is good for most objects, while black works well for jewelry and sometimes glass. Some sellers like a neutral gray, which also works well for most craft items.

FIGURE 4.6

Hang some sort of seamless photographic background behind your item to make it pop in the picture.

The background, of course, can and probably should also function as the base beneath the item you're shooting. That is, the items you're photographing should be placed on top of the background material, which then sweeps upward behind the items. This way, you get a seamless transition from "floor" to the back wall, with nothing to detract from the craft itself.

> **NOTE** You can find photographic backgrounds, auxiliary lighting, and tripods at your local camera supply store, or at online photo stores.

CONSIDERING A LIGHT TENT FOR SMALLER ITEMS

Since many craft items are somewhat small, you can create great product photos by shooting the item inside a *light tent*. This is an enclosure with white sides, some of which are translucent, into which you insert the item to be shot. A light shines from outside the box or tent through the translucent wall(s), just providing diffused lighting inside the enclosure. (Your camera typically shoots through an open side, or through a hole in one of the sides.)

NOTE A light tent is sometimes called a light box or soft box.

You can make your own light tent out of a plain white milk jug, or a white plastic bowl, or a white sheet. Anything white and translucent will work. If you're using a milk jug, cut the bottom off and place the jug over your subject. Illuminate from the sides and shoot through the open spout of the jug.

You can make a larger light tent just by draping a sheet or other white material over and around a table. Another option is to glue sheets of styrofoam together into a cube form, with the bottom left open—and then shoot through the open end.

Or, if you don't want to go through all that trouble, you can buy a preassembled light tent from companies such as Square Perfect, CowboyStudio, and Smith-Victor. Figure 4.7 shows CowboyStudio's Table Top Photo Studio Light Tent, which includes a compact 16" × 16" × 16" cube, two 50-watt external lights, and an adjustable-height camera stand. It comes with four different background colors and sells for under $40—a very affordable alternative when you're photographing small crafts.

FIGURE 4.7

CowboyStudio's all-in-one light tent kit, complete with lights and camera stand. (www.cowboystudio.com)

FIXING THE FLAWS WITH PHOTO EDITING SOFTWARE

The final item you need to create great-looking photos of your crafts is a photo editing software program for your computer. We'll talk more about these programs and what you can do with them later in this chapter, but suffice to say that you need a photo editing program to fix any flaws in your photos, crop them to size, and put a little extra sheen on reality. In other words, a photo editing program helps to make your photos look better, after the fact.

There are a lot of photo editing programs out there, some free and some tremendously expensive. (Adobe Photoshop CS, used by many professional photographers, falls into the latter category.) You don't need anything too fancy—something affordable that's easy to use and includes all the image editing features you need to create quality product photos.

There are a number of easy-to-use, low-cost programs available. The most popular of these programs include the following:

- Adobe Photoshop Elements (www.adobe.com), $99.99

- Paint Shop Photo Express Pro (www.corel.com), $79.99

- Photo Explosion Deluxe (www.novadevelopment.com), $49.95

- Picasa (picasa.google.com), free

As you can see, all of these programs cost under $100 and have similar features. I personally use Picasa, shown in Figure 4.8, but any of these programs should do the job for you.

FIGURE 4.8

Use Picasa or a similar photo editing program to put the finishing touches on your product photos.

HOW TO TAKE GREAT PRODUCT PHOTOS

Once you have the proper equipment, it's time to take a few photos. A good product photo is almost identical to an artistic still life, and requires the same set of skills. You need good lighting to show off the product, and to highlight its details (both good and bad—you need to show the flaws as well). The photo has to represent the item to potential customers online, so it needs to be both accurate and flattering.

You'll get the best results when you pay particular attention to the lighting. You should always use diffuse light from an angle; never use your camera's built-in flash. (The flash will create glare off of shiny surfaces; it's particularly bad when shooting shrink-wrapped items.) And always mount your camera on a tripod; it's the best way to ensure against blurry photos.

Don't worry too much about artistic composition. The key thing to remember is that your craft needs to be big in the frame. This means getting the camera physically close to the item, or using a slight zoom to accomplish the same effect. For smaller products, this may mean using your camera's macro mode.

When creating photos for online viewing, don't obsess over high resolution. The photos displayed on Etsy or eBay are big enough to display comfortably in a web browser but no bigger than that. Whether you do it in the camera or afterward in a photo editing program, reduce the resolution to no more than 2000 × 2000 pixels, and a little lower is probably okay.

Make sure the product stands out by using a plain black, white, or gray background behind and beneath the item. That doesn't mean that a product photo has to be boring, however. If it's a grayish, visually boring item, it's okay to put it against a brightly colored background. For that matter, there's no rule against accessorizing the item with a brightly colored item. Use your imagination, and remember that the photos are being used to *sell* the item. You want to make that product as appealing as possible.

Finally, while it's okay to adjust brightness and color to a small degree in Photoshop, it's not a good idea to perform wholesale touchups after the fact. Customers want to see what the product really looks like, not a vision of the ideal product. Use Photoshop to correct for poor shooting conditions, not to touch up flaws in the product.

WORKING WITH LIGHTING

I've talked a bit about lighting throughout this chapter because lighting is important. It may be the single most important factor in making a good photo look great.

While you can use natural lighting (by shooting outdoors on an slightly overcast day, to avoid direct shadows), you'll show off your crafts to better effect by shooting indoors with external lighting—*not* with your camera's built-in flash. The ideal setup, shown in Figure 4.9, uses two external lights, each positioned at 45-degree angles to the camera-to-subject axis.

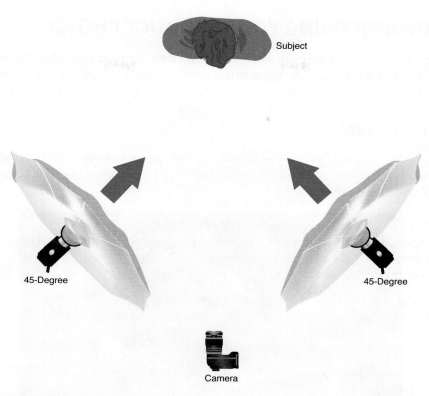

FIGURE 4.9

The recommended lighting setup for product photos.

You'll get even better results by using some sort of diffuser or softbox on each light flood. This puts a nice soft light on all the parts of the item, more or less equally.

> **NOTE** A softbox is a translucent fabric "box" that attaches directly to a photoflood, serving to diffuse or soften the source light.

If you don't have external lights, you can use a speed light attached to your camera, instead. The key here is to configure the speed light for bounce lighting; bounce the light off the ceiling above you or the wall behind. On no condition should you use the direct lighting of your camera's built-in flash.

TIPS FOR IMPROVING YOUR PRODUCT PHOTOS

The best craft photos online are those that show off the items to best effect. To that end, here are some tips to help you shoot better product photos—which should result in higher sales.

CENTER THE ITEM

To take effective photographs, you have to learn proper composition. That means centering the item in the center of the frame. Don't position your craft off-center, as in Figure 4.10; that just wastes space!

FIGURE 4.10
The framing is artistic but wastes space on the page—the item should be centered and cropped instead.

MAKE IT LARGE

You want your craft to fill up the entire picture, so that your customers can best see what you're selling. That means getting close enough to the item (or using your camera's zoom lens) so that it fills up the entire frame, and getting close enough to the object so that it fills up the entire picture. Don't stand halfway across the room and shoot a very small object; get close up and make it big!

> **TIP** If you don't get close enough to fill the frame, you can always crop the photo in the editing process to eliminate unused space around the edges.

SHOOT AT AN ANGLE

You should take your photo in front of your craft—but not literally the front. Most items are a tad more appealing when shot from a slight angle. Instead of moving the camera, turn the item so that you're shooting a 3/4 profile, as shown in Figure 4.11.

FIGURE 4.11
Shoot your craft at a slight angle, not head on.

SHOOT MULTIPLE PHOTOS

For most crafts you sell, you want to take more than one photo. Photograph the item from the angled front, of course, but if the sides and top are important, angle the item (or move the camera) to shoot them, as well. You may also want to shoot close ups of any product details—the inset of a ring or bracelet, for example, or the stitching on a quilt or sweater. Photograph anything that's important to potential customers.

> ✂ **TIP** You should also closely photograph any flaws in your item. It's important for customers to see both the good and the bad of the product, in extreme detail.

AVOID GLARE

If you're shooting a glass or plastic item, or an item in plastic wrap or similar packaging, or just an item that's naturally shiny, you have to work hard to avoid glare from whatever lighting source you're using. This is one reason why I typically don't recommend using a single-point flash—without any fill lighting, it produces too much glare. You avoid glare by not using a flash, adding fill lighting (to the sides of the object), diffusing the lighting source (by using a softbox or bouncing the light off a reflector or nearby wall), or just turning the item until the glare goes away. Just beware of the glare problem, and somehow compensate for it.

ACCESSORIZE YOUR PHOTOS

Add some seasonal interest to your craft photos by adding appropriate props and accessories to the picture, as shown in Figure 4.12. If you're selling homemade candy, include a fancy plate or candy jar. If you're selling handcrafted baskets, fill the baskets with colorful fruit and vegetables. You get the idea.

FIGURE 4.12

If you're selling fruit baskets, photograph them with colorful fruit inside! (Photo courtesy Etsy shop CharestStudios)

Props can also add some seasonal fun to your photos. During the Christmas season, shoot your items next to a small Christmas tree or fake snowman. At Halloween, use a jack o' lantern as a prop. During the hot summer months, have a bikini model pose with your item. (Okay, maybe that last suggestion is a bit overboard... unless you're selling swimwear, that is.) In any case, use props to make your photos stand out—whatever the season.

SHOOTING DIFFERENT TYPES OF CRAFTS

As you might suspect, different types of crafts offer different challenges in terms of creating effective product photos. Let's take a look a few of the more popular types of crafts and what you need to keep in mind, photographically speaking.

SHOOTING CLEAR OR TRANSLUCENT GLASS

You want to illuminate glass items from the rear and sides, or from the top, as shown in Figure 4.13. Clear or translucent glass often requires more than one light to look best. You can use either a light or dark background, depending on the characteristics of the glass. Faceted or cut glass usually looks best against a dark background.

FIGURE 4.13

Illuminate glass items from the rear and sides. (And there's nothing wrong with filling up a glass with colorful liquid, either.)

SHOOTING OPAQUE GLASS AND JEWELRY

Shooting opaque glass, jewelry, and silver items is somewhat difficult because of all the potential reflections. To avoid reflections and harsh highlights, you want a very broad, diffused light. The easiest way to get this is to use a translucent light tent around your subject. You then leave a hole for your camera lens to poke through and illuminate the tent evenly from at least two sides.

SHOOTING WOOD ITEMS

The challenge with shooting any high-gloss wood craft is glare. The first thing to do is to *not* use your camera's flash; this will cause the wood to glare back at you from every highlight, and it won't show the shape of the item well. Better to use diffused light from a photoflood, to get enough light onto the woodgrain. You can also shoot the item in natural light, from a window or by shooting outdoors.

SHOOTING CLOTHING

Shooting clothing requires a lot of light. This is where the recommended two-light setup comes in, providing two strong light sources that highlight all the folds of the cloth. If you can, diffuse the lights to soften any shadows—and never use flash!

CAUTION One potential problem with shooting colored fabrics is that most digital cameras are very sensitive to otherwise-invisible infrared light—and fabrics, especially synthetic ones, reflect a lot of infrared. This can result in a subtle color shift that doesn't accurately reproduce the fabric's colors. The only real solution to this problem is to correct the colors after the shoot, using image-editing software.

Fabrics with strong lines or checks present an additional problem, in the form of moiré patterns. This is caused when two interfering patterns overlap—in this case, the pattern of the fabric vs. the pattern of pixels in your digital image. You may be able to lessen or eliminate the moiré effect by shooting at a different distance or with the camera at a slight angle to the subject.

If you're selling an item with black or dark fabric, the challenge is being able to pull detail out of the darkness. You have to step up the lighting to create shadows and highlights on the fabric.

Then there's the matter of how to display clothing in your photos. The best approach here is to use a mannequin or clothing form to display items of clothing. As you can see in Figure 4.14, hanging the clothing on a mannequin lets potential buyers see what the item looks like in real life; it's much better than the "ghost effect" you get by shooting clothing lying flat on the floor.

FIGURE 4.14

Display clothing on a mannequin or clothing form. (Photo courtesy Etsy shop klassicline.)

Even better is to use a model to display your clothing and accessories, as shown in Figure 4.15. You probably don't have the funds to hire a professional model, but friends and family members can help you model your clothing for the camera. If you know someone who's adequately photogenic, get out the makeup and start shooting.

FIGURE 4.15

Have an attractive model wear your clothing. (Photo courtesy Etsy shop subrosa123)

TIP Models are also great for displaying jewelry. A pretty necklace or bracelet looks better fitted around a real human being than hanging off a dull mannequin.

SCANNING FLAT AND SMALL ITEMS

If you're selling relatively flat items (paintings, pins, and other artwork), you might be better off with a scanner than a camera. Just lay the object on a flatbed scanner and scan the item into a file on your computer. It's actually easier to scan some items than it is to take a good steady picture!

The scanner trick isn't just for flat items. It can also work, in a pinch, for small items, such as jewelry. In fact, some sellers swear by scanning jewelry, claiming that detail is somewhat sharper with a scanner than with a typical digital camera. It certainly doesn't hurt to try it.

EDITING YOUR PHOTOS—DIGITALLY

When you're taking a digital photo, you want to save your images in the JPG file format. This is the default file format for most digital cameras, although some devices give you a choice of other formats (TIF, camera raw, and so on). The JPG format is the de facto standard for web images and what eBay, Etsy, and similar sites expect for your craft listings. Given the choice, choose JPG.

With your photos in JPG format, you can easily touch them up with digital photo editing software. Now, if you're a perfect photographer, you may never need to touch up the pictures you take. But since most of us are far from perfect, it's great to be able to "punch up" the photos we take—and make them as perfect as possible for our item listings.

Just what can or should you touch up in your digital photos? Here's a short list:

- **Brightness and contrast.** If you don't use the right kind of lighting, you can end up with a shot that's too dark or too light. This is a problem some less-careful crafters have when shooting quick-and-dirty shots for online use. Fortunately, you can use any photo editing program to fix these problems without a lot of fuss and bother, by adjusting the appropriate brightness, contrast, or levels controls.

- **Color and tint.** The wrong lighting can also affect a picture's white balance, resulting in oversaturated colors or off-tint hues. Use your photo editing program's various color and tint/hue controls to achieve a more natural color balance.

■ **Cropping.** If you didn't get close enough to your subject, or if you framed it incorrectly, you can correct the problem by cropping the picture in your photo editing program. Use the crop control to remove the unwanted edges and put your craft front and center in the frame, as shown in Figure 4.16.

■ **Reducing image size.** A high megapixel camera will create photos that are larger than necessary for online viewing. For example, an 8 megapixel image creates a 4" × 6" image that's 2448 pixels high by 3264 pixels wide. You don't need much more than 2000 pixels at the largest dimension, so you can use your photo editing software to resize the image and reduce the file size.

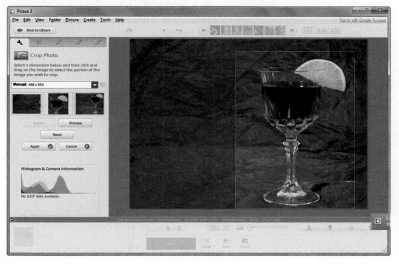

FIGURE 4.16

Cropping a photo with Picasa.

You can't turn a lousy picture into a great one, but you can use a photo editing program to make a good picture look a little better. Every little bit helps; remember, you're trying to put the best face on your crafts for potential customers to see.

Deciding Where to Sell Online

5

Now that you know how to sell your crafts online, the challenge becomes *where* to do so. There are dozens of websites that offer listings from crafters and other artisans, as well as big general marketplaces, such as eBay and Amazon. And you can always bypass the marketplaces completely and sell your goods direct to consumers on your own website.

Which website is the best for selling your own specific crafts? There's no one right answer to that question and, in fact, you may find that you want to sell your crafts on multiple online marketplaces. That's great, you can do that, although for smaller sellers it may be better to focus your efforts on a single site. But which site should you choose?

Read on to learn more.

SELLING ON DEDICATED ONLINE CRAFT MARKETPLACES

The first place you may want to consider for selling your crafts is a dedicated online craft marketplace—that is, a website that specializes in connecting craft sellers with craft buyers. These sites don't offer much of anything beyond crafts; these are not sites someone would visit to buy general consumer items.

Just as there are hundreds, if not thousands, of physical arts and craft marketplaces across the U.S., there are dozens and dozens of these online craft marketplaces on the Internet. Some, such as Etsy and ArtFire, are pretty big, hosting thousands of individual merchants; others are much smaller, kind of like your local arts mall, with only a few hundred merchants (or less).

Most online craft marketplaces work in much the same fashion. You, the crafter, opens an online shop or store within the marketplace. Your shop gets its own URL (web address) and you can customize the shop's home page to some degree. You post listings for the crafts you have for sale, and they're featured both in your store and within the larger site when someone searches or browses for that kind of craft. When a customer purchases one of your items, it's paid for via the payment processing system (such as PayPal) provided by the craft site.

To be included in one of these craft sites, you have to pay a few fees. You'll typically pay a listing fee (a one-time fee for listing each item), a selling fee (call it a commission, a percentage of the final sales price when an item is sold), and a payment processing fee (another percentage of the sales price, for processing the customer's payment). Naturally, you only pay selling and payment processing fees when you make a sale; the only money you're out upfront is the listing fees for each item listed.

> **NOTE** Some online marketplaces also charge you a flat monthly fee to maintain your online storefront.

Space prohibits us from discussing each and every craft marketplace on the web; there really are that many of them. We'll focus our efforts on those sites that operate within the United States (thus excluding U.K.-only sites, for example) and only on the most popular of these sites.

ETSY

Speaking of popular, the single most popular craft-specific marketplace on the Internet today is Etsy (www.etsy.com). Etsy claims more than 15 million members and more than 875,000 active sellers/shops. On any given day you'll find more than 7 million items listed; the site does more than $300 million in gross sales a year. That's pretty big, folks; no other dedicated craft site comes close.

> **NOTE** Learn more about selling crafts on Etsy in Chapter 6, "Selling on Etsy."

As you can see in Figure 5.1, Etsy is a very visual site, kind of like Pinterest but for buying and selling crafts. Etsy organizes its crafts into a dozen or so major categories (Accessories, Art, Bags and Purses, Bath and Beauty, and so forth), each with its own unique subcategories. Customers can also search for specific types of crafts.

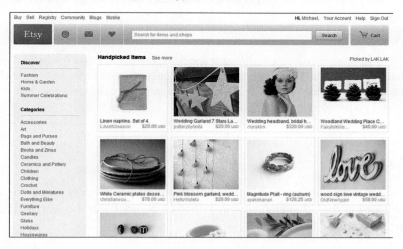

FIGURE 5.1

Etsy, the Internet's largest crafts-only marketplace.

To sell on Etsy, you have to offer goods in one of the following three categories:

- Handmade (anything you personally craft or construct)
- Vintage (20 years or older)
- Supplies, such as beads, jewelry-making tools, and the like

Etsy's fees aren't nothing, but they are lower than what you find with eBay, for instance. It costs a flat $0.20 to list an item, and you pay Etsy 3.5% of the final selling price, not including shipping fees or tax. If an item doesn't sell, you're only out the initial twenty cents.

> **NOTE** You pay $0.20 per listing, no matter what quantity you have for sale. But when you sell one item from a multiple-quantity listing, Etsy automatically renews the listing for a new $0.20 listing fee.

A listing is good for four months or until the item is sold, whichever comes first. If an item doesn't sell during that time frame, you can renew the listing for another $0.20. In addition, you'll pay 3% of the amount paid plus $0.25 per item for payment processing, using Etsy's direct checkout system.

Many crafters like Etsy because of its crafts-only focus, which brings a very targeted audience to the site. That's in direct comparison to eBay, which has (much) more traffic but doesn't have that crafts-only focus. As such, it's easier to build a presence and connect with a like-minded community on Etsy than it is with eBay and other general sites.

> **TIP** For many sellers, the most appealing thing about Etsy is that it's a true community of arts and crafts lovers. Etsy buyers value handmade items, and know what to expect; eBay buyers don't always. That makes Etsy a more personal place to do business, which may matter to you.

ARTBREAK

Etsy is the big dog in online craft marketplaces, but it's not the only pup in the pack. As such, we'll look at the other craft sites in alphabetical order, starting with Artbreak (www.artbreak.com).

As you can see in Figure 5.2, Artbreak is an online marketplace for art and artists. You can sell artwork within any of the site's designated categories: Paintings and Drawings, Prints, Photography, Mixed Media, Clothing, Sculpture, Furniture, Ceramics and Glass, Wood and Fiber, and Jewelry.

Interestingly, Artbreak charges no listing or commission fees; the site is free. All sales, however, must be made directly between sellers and buyers, as Artbreak provides no shopping cart or payment processing system.

ARTFIRE

ArtFire (www.artfire.com), is probably the number-two online crafts marketplace, after Etsy. As you can see in Figure 5.3, ArtFire offers arts and crafts for sale in the following major categories: Handmade, Design, Supplies, Media, Vintage, Fine Art, and Commercial. Under Handmade, you find a plethora of subcategories, such as Accessories, Bags and Purses, Baskets, Bath and Beauty, Candles, and the like.

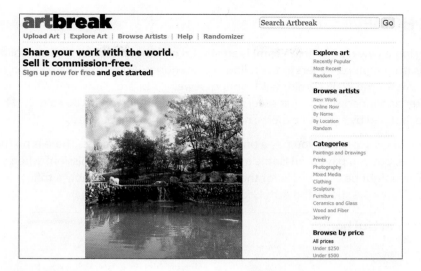

FIGURE 5.2

Artbreak, an online marketplace for art and artists.

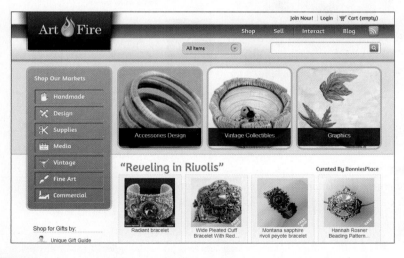

FIGURE 5.3

ArtFire charges a flat monthly fee with no per-transaction fees.

Unlike Etsy, which charges per-item and per-transaction fees, ArtFire charges sellers a flat $12.95 a month for online storefronts. You can choose from PayPal, ProPay, and Amazon Payments for your payment processing.

ARTFUL HOME

Artful Home (www.artfulhome.com) is an art and crafts marketplace that consolidates listings from multiple sellers in the following categories: Art Glass, Ceramics, Objects & Décor, Art for the Wall, Furniture & Lighting, Jewelry, Apparel, Gifts, and What's New. It operates as a juried site, in that sellers must apply for their work to be sold, and have their work examined by a jury of experts; not all applications are accepted.

If your work is accepted, you pay a one-time $300 membership fee. There is no further listing fee, but you pay Artful Home a 50% "standard gallery commission" when your work sells. That might be acceptable for the fine art market, but is probably a trifle pricy for craft sellers. (Figure 5.4 shows the Artful Home home page.)

FIGURE 5.4

Artful Home, a juried marketplace for handmade art.

NOTE A juried marketplace requires potential sellers to submit their artwork or crafts before you can sell on the site. You may be required to pay a submittal or jury fee. (Artful Home charges $35 per application.) The site's jury or panel of experts will review your application, and let you know if your work is accepted to be sold on the site. (Not all submissions are accepted.)

ARTIST RISING

Artist Rising (www.artistrising.com) is an offshoot of the popular Art.com site, designed for sales of original art and prints by member artists. At present, the site offers more than 300,000 works from more than 55,000 different artists.

As you can see in Figure 5.5, artwork is organized into a number of logical categories, such as Abstract, Animals, Architecture, and the like. If you want to sell your work, you need to have a membership; free membership lets you offer 50 different items, while the $50/year Premium membership gives you 2,000 slots. Either way, the site pays you a 30% royalty on each item of yours they sell. (Looking at this another way, you pay a 70% commission on each item sold—a little on the pricy side.)

FIGURE 5.5

Artist Rising, which sells original art and prints from rising artists.

ARTSPAN

Artspan (www.artspan.com) is a marketplace that hosts more than 4,000 custom member websites. You pay anywhere from $13.95 to $19.95 per month for Artspan to host your site; you can then offer any of your own artwork on the site, with no listing or commission fees. Potential customers can then search Artspan by type of art, location, or artist to find what they're looking for. (Figure 5.6 shows a typical artist site on Artspan.)

FIGURE 5.6
AnimalCoin's Artspan website (animalcoin.artspan.com), selling handpainted coin jewelry.

BONANZA

Bonanza (www.bonanza.com) is a marketplace offering clothing, crafts, collectibles, health and beauty items, home and garden products, and jewelry and watches from individual sellers. The site claims more than 3 million items listed for sale, with more than 3 million site visitors per month.

> **NOTE** Bonanza was formerly known as Bonanzle, but was renamed in 2010 "as a tribute to the late Pernell Roberts, known to millions as 'Adam Cartwright' from the TV western series *Bonanza*." Really.

As you see in Figure 5.7, Bonanza looks more like an online retailer than a typical online marketplace, at least to initial shoppers. Once you get to the product listings, however, it's clear that customers are buying from individual sellers.

As to costs, Bonanza's selling fee (they call it a Final Offer Value fee) is 3.5% of the final selling price for items priced under $500, with a $0.50 minimum. There's no initial listing fee.

CRAFT IS ART

Craft is Art (www.craftisart.com), shown in Figure 5.8, is an artisan marketplace for handmade and vintage items. It's a flat price marketplace for sellers; you pay $9.99 per month with no listing or selling fees. You do, however, have to pay fees to whichever payment processing service (such as PayPal) you choose to use.

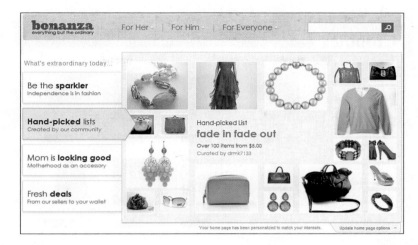

FIGURE 5.7

The Bonanza online marketplace.

FIGURE 5.8

The Craft is Art marketplace for handmade items.

> **NOTE**   Craft is Art also offers a "free" pay-as-you-go plan that costs you $1.00 per listing and a 4.5% commission on each sale made.

CROBBIES

Crobbies (www.crobbies.com) is a marketplace for handmade items from individual sellers. As you can see in Figure 5.9, you can sell items in a variety of craft categories, from Art/Painting and Bags and Purses to Weddings and Woodworking.

FIGURE 5.9

Crobbies, an online marketplace for handmade crafts and hobbies.

You create your own Crobbies shop and then list the items you have for sale. Crobbies' per-item plan charges a $0.15 per item listing fee and a 3% selling fee. The Unlimited Monthly Plan costs a flat $7.95 per month, but doesn't charge any listing or selling fees.

> **NOTE**   The word "crobbies" is a combination of the words "crafts" and "hobbies."

FUNKY FINDS

Funky Finds (www.funkyfinds.com) is a smallish online marketplace for independent artists, crafters, and designers. Customers shop The Shops @ Funky Finds, shown in Figure 5.10, where they can search or browse by category.

The site charges no listing or selling fees. Instead, you pay to create your own online shop; fees range from $5.97 to $23.97 per four-month period, depending on how many listings you want to include.

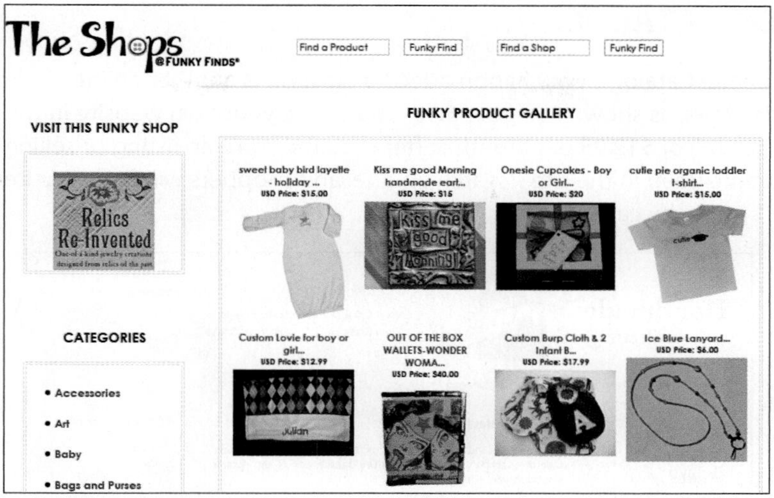

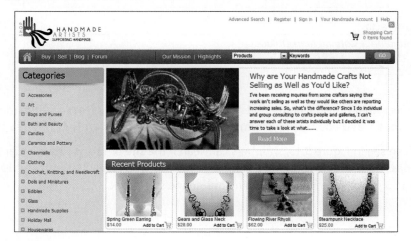

FIGURE 5.10
Item listings at The Shops @ Funky Finds.

HANDMADE ARTISTS SHOP

The Handmade Artists Shop (www.handmadeartists.com) is an online marketplace for all manner of handmade art and crafts. (Figure 5.11 shows the website.) You pay $5 per month to set up your online shop; after that, there are no listing or sales fees.

FIGURE 5.11
The Handmade Artists Shop.

HANDMADE CATALOG

The Handmade Catalog (www.handmadecatalog.com) is another online marketplace for handmade crafts, as shown in Figure 5.12. You create your own website in the marketplace (for $4.95, $7.95, or $12.95 per month); after that, there are no listing or selling fees. Your listings get included in the site's search engine, and shoppers will find your items when they search or browse by category.

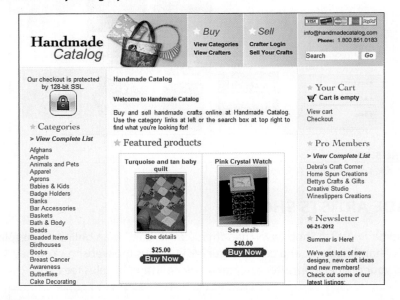

FIGURE 5.12

The Handmade Catalog marketplace.

HYENA CART

Despite its rather unusual name, Hyena Cart (www.hyenacart.com) is a standard marketplace for handmade (and eco-friendly) items. The site boasts more than 1,000 unique stores.

As you can see in Figure 5.13, shoppers can search the site or browse by standard craft categories. There are no listing or selling fees; instead, you pay a $10 initial setup fee and an ongoing $5 per month fee to maintain your online storefront.

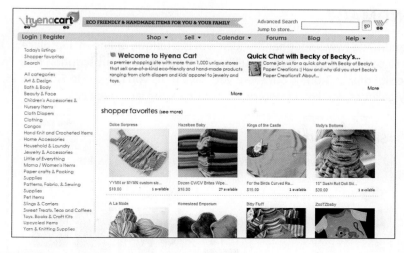

FIGURE 5.13

The Hyena Cart online marketplace.

MADE IT MYSELF

Made It Myself (www.madeitmyself.com) is yet another marketplace for handmade items in the standard categories. (Figure 5.14 shows the site's home page.) The site doesn't charge any listing fees; selling fees are 3% of the final selling price.

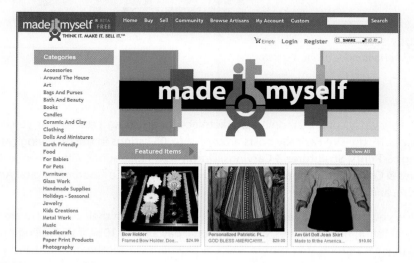

FIGURE 5.14

The Made It Myself marketplace for handmade goods.

SHOPHANDMADE

ShopHandmade (www.shophandmade.com) is a unique online marketplace in that there are no fees to pay—no listing fees, no selling fees, no monthly subscription fees. I'm not sure how the site makes money, but there you have it. As you can see in Figure 5.15, visitors can shop by galleries, market, keywords, categories, store, and even color.

FIGURE 5.15

The ShopHandmade online marketplace.

YESSY

Yessy (www.yessy.com) is an online marketplace for artists and crafters. As you can see in Figure 5.16, the site typically hosts around 150,000 listings in the following categories: Paintings & Prints, Sculptures & Carvings, Drawings & Illustrations, Glass, Textile & Apparel, Antiques & Collectibles, Photography, Ceramics & Pottery, Computer & Digital Art, Jewelry, Furniture, and Crafts & Other Art.

Fee-wise, you pay $59 per year for the privilege of selling on their site. There are no additional listing or selling fees, although you'll pay a hefty 10% of the selling price if you use Yessy's payment processing system. (Accept payment via another method and you don't pay this fee.)

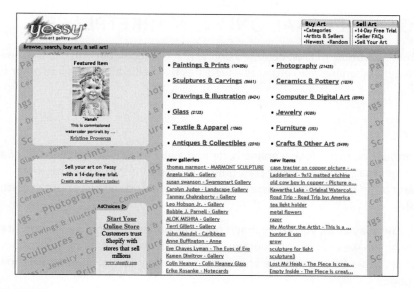

FIGURE 5.16
The Yessy online marketplace.

ZIBBET

Zibbet (www.zibbet.com), shown in Figure 5.17, is a marketplace for handmade products. There's no upfront or listing fees; when you sell an item, you pay a 7.5% selling fee.

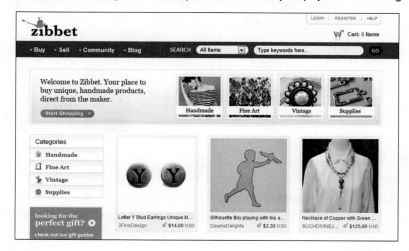

FIGURE 5.17
The Zibbet marketplace for handmade items.

SELLING ON GENERAL ONLINE MARKETPLACES

Okay, that's a bundle of craft-centered online marketplaces. But you can also sell your crafts in more general online marketplaces—websites that sell crafts alongside other types of products.

EBAY

The number-one marketplace online is, far and away, eBay (www.ebay.com). eBay is much, much larger than Etsy and other craft-only sites, in part because it offers more than just crafts and other handmade items; everybody can buy and sell just about everything on the eBay site.

If you know eBay at all, you know that it made its bones as an online auction site. While auctions still make up a fair percentage of its listings, the majority of listings today are at a fixed price, either for a fixed time or in individuals' eBay Stores. (Figure 5.18 shows eBay's home page.)

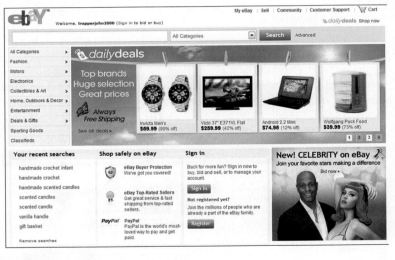

FIGURE 5.18

eBay, the web's largest online marketplace.

As a craft seller, you'll probably want to use eBay's fixed-price listings—unless, that is, you have a very rare or collectible item that can fetch a better price by going to the highest bidder. Most craft sellers, however, find that setting a fixed price for their work is easier and brings better results.

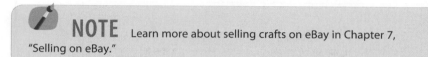

NOTE Learn more about selling crafts on eBay in Chapter 7, "Selling on eBay."

What eBay does well is deliver a huge amount of traffic to your virtual door. Where Etsy, the biggest craft-only site, claims to have around 12 million registered users, eBay has more than 200 million users. That's a lot of potential customers for your handmade crafts.

Of course, you have to pay for that additional traffic. eBay charges $0.50 for a typical seven-day listing, and a whopping 11% final selling fee. (The listing fee is only $0.20 if you have an eBay Store, however—but the final value fee is the same.) That's considerably more than what you pay at Etsy.

So here's what you get with eBay compared to craft-only sites: more traffic (which presumably translates into higher sales) and higher fees. Is it a good trade-off? We'll discuss that later in this chapter.

CRAIGSLIST

What about Craigslist? If you're not familiar with Craigslist (www.craigslist.org), it's essentially a site for classified advertising. As such, Craigslist listings are localized; when you want to sell something, you create an ad and post it to your local Craigslist site.

As you can see in Figure 5.19, Craigslist has all sorts of classified listings for everything from employment and personals to housing and items for sale. Naturally, you'd post a listing for your crafts in the For Sale category, under the appropriate subcategory.

Now, Craigslist is a big deal if you're selling certain types of items—used furniture and appliances, lawn mowers and musical instruments, that sort of thing. But it's not so great for selling handmade crafts, although you're certainly free to test it out for yourself.

Crafters simply haven't had much luck selling on Craigslist. There are probably a number of reasons for this.

First off, most shoppers on Craigslist are looking for specific items (furniture, appliances, whatever), and for a really good deal on those items. They're not necessarily on Craigslist looking for handmade art and crafts.

Second, you really can't create a lasting presence for yourself on the Craigslist site. You create individual listings for each item you have for sale, but each listing gets pushed further down the list each day it's active, by newer listings from other users. There's no personalized store to "park" your items at; it's listings only, and you have to keep relisting them to ensure they get noticed on the site.

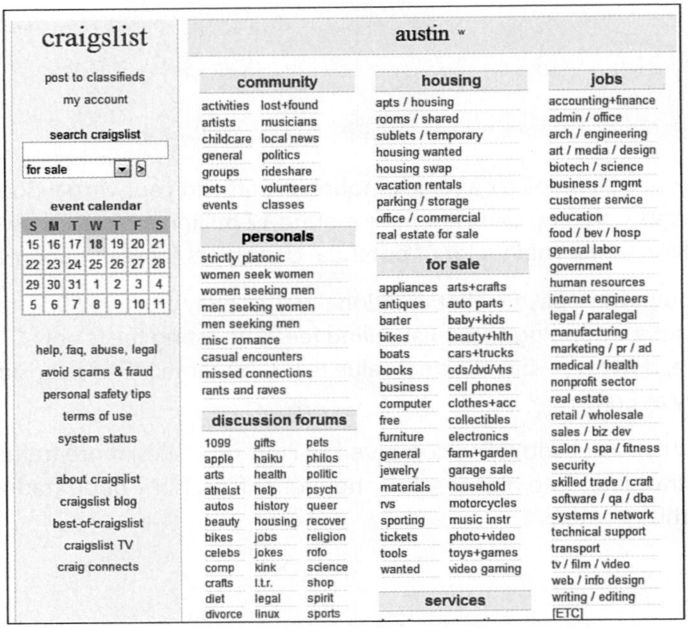

FIGURE 5.19

Craigslist, an online classified advertising site.

Third, unlike all the other marketplaces we've discussed, Craigslist search results do not display thumbnail images; someone searching or browsing the site only sees text titles and prices. Given how image-reliant the art/craft market is, this is a huge issue. How can someone be enticed to view your craft if she can't see it in the listings?

Not to say that there aren't some appealing things about Craigslist. Okay, one appealing thing—the price. All Craigslist listings are free—no listing fees and no selling fees. You don't have to pay anyone when you sell an item. That's great.

The downside is that Craigslist doesn't offer any of the selling services you find on Etsy, eBay, and similar sites. When someone finds something she wants to buy, she has to contact the seller directly, via email. All correspondence is between the buyer and seller, not through the Craigslist site. And when the sale goes down, the buyer pays the seller directly—there is no on-site payment processing of any sort. It really is like the old newspaper classified ads, just online.

That's why so few crafters have found Craigslist either appealing or successful. You may think different, but that's the way it looks from here.

ECRATER

eCRATER (www.ecrater.com) is a mix of a web store building service and online marketplace. That is, eCRATER helps you build and then hosts your own online shop, and then feeds your products into its own online marketplace. Consumers can search and browse the marketplace for specific items, as you see in Figure 5.20; they're then taken directly to sellers' stores to learn more and hopefully complete the purchase.

FIGURE 5.20

eCRATER, a store hosting service and online marketplace.

As such, eCRATER is more than just a craft marketplace. eCRATER hosts merchants in a variety of consumer categories, from baby toys to watches. Naturally, art and crafts are two of the main categories in the marketplace.

The nice thing about eCRATER is that it's free for sellers. You don't pay any hosting, listing, or selling fees; you keep every dollar you make. That's attractive.

RUBY LANE

Ruby Lane (www.rubylane.com) is a well-established marketplace for art, jewelry, antiques, and vintage collectibles. As you can see in Figure 5.21, that includes a fair amount of crafts, even though the site is not exclusively devoted to handmade items.

This site's fee schedule is a little confusing. You pay a one-time $75 setup fee to open your Ruby Lane shop, and then an ongoing $20/month advertising fee. You also pay a $0.30 per item listing fee, as well as an ongoing $0.30 per month maintenance fee for each item listed. You do not, however, pay any selling fees when you sell an item.

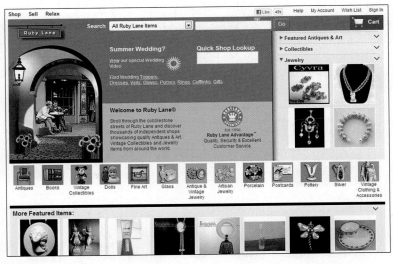

FIGURE 5.21

Ruby Lane, a general online marketplace with a heavy focus on art and crafts.

SILKFAIR

SilkFair (www.silkfair.com) is another general online marketplace with a heavy art and craft focus. Figure 5.22 shows the SilkFair site; categories include both Arts and Crafts, as well as Automotive, Beauty & Fragrances, Flowers & Gifts, Glass & Pottery, Jewelry & Accessories, Real Estate, Tools & Hardwares, and more.

You can sign up for SilkFair at one of six selling levels, from Market Booth (no subscription fees) to Unlimited ($24.99 per month). There are no listing fees, but you do pay a 3% selling fee on all items sold.

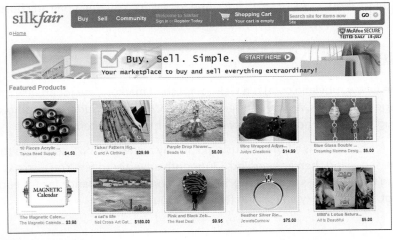

FIGURE 5.22

The SilkFair general online marketplace.

COMPARING THE TOP ONLINE MARKETPLACES

Okay, so that's 22 potential online marketplaces for your handmade crafts. How do you choose the one that's right for you? Or should you choose more than one?

The first thing to do is to look at all the data in one place, so you can easily compare site type, fees, and so forth. This is what we do in Table 5.1; hope it's not too confusing.

Table 5.1   Major Online Marketplaces

Marketplace	URL	Type	Setup Fee	Monthly Fee	Listing Fee	Selling Fee (Commission)
Artbreak	www.artbreak.com	Art marketplace	None	None	None	None
ArtFire	www.artfire.com	Crafts marketplace	None	$12.95	None	None
Artful Home	www.artfulhome.com	Juried art and crafts marketplace	$300	No	None	50%
Artist Rising	www.artistrising.com	Art marketplace	None	$0/$50 yearly	None	70%
Artspan	www.artspan.com	Art marketplace	None	$13.95–$19.95	None	None
Bonanza	www.bonanza.com	Craft marketplace	None	None	None	3.5%
Craft is Art	www.craftisart.com	Artisan marketplace for handmade items	None	None/$9.99	$1.00/none	4.5%/none
Craigslist	www.craigslist.com	General online classifieds	None	None	None	None
Crobbies	www.crobbies.com	Handmade craft marketplace	None	None/$7.95	$0.15/none	3%/none
eBay	www.ebay.com	General online marketplace (includes online auctions)	None	None (eBay Store subscription fees run $15.95 and up)	$0.50 ($0.20 for eBay Store listings)	11%
eCRATER	www.ecrater.com	General online marketplace	None	None	None	None
Etsy	www.etsy.com	Art and crafts marketplace	None	None	$0.20	3.5%
Funky Finds	www.funkyfinds.com	Art, craft, and design marketplace	None	$5.97–$23.97 (four-month period)	None	None
Handmade Artists Shop	www. handmadeartists.com	Art and crafts marketplace	None	$5.00	None	None
Handmade Catalog	www. handmadecatalog.com	Handmade crafts marketplace	None	$4.95–$12.95	None	None

Table 5.1   **Major Online Marketplaces**   continued

Marketplace	URL	Type	Setup Fee	Monthly Fee	Listing Fee	Selling Fee (Commission)
Hyena Cart	www.hyenacart.com	Handmade marketplace	$10	$5	None	None
Made It Myself	www.madeitmyself.com	Handmade marketplace	None	None	None	3%
Ruby Lane	www.rubylane.com	General online marketplace	$75	$20	$0.30	None
ShopHandmade	www.shophandmade.com	Handmade marketplace	None	None	None	None
SilkFair	www.silkfair.com	General online marketplace	None	$0–$24.99	None	3%
Yessy	www.yessy.com	Arts and crafts marketplace	None	$59/year	None	None
Zibbet	www.zibbet.com	Handmade marketplace	None	None	None	7.5%

EXAMINING IMPORTANT FACTORS

That's a lot of options. How do you choose the site that's best for you?

There are a number of factors to consider—focus, size, and cost probably most important. Let's look at each in turn.

TYPE OF SITE

As an artist or crafter, you may want to feature your work on a site that's specific to your field of interest. That guarantees you a focused audience; you won't be selling paintings to plumbers or beads to babysitters.

As such, that would argue in favor of sites such as Etsy and ArtFire (for crafters) or Artist Rising and ArtSpan (for artists), over general sites like eBay and Ruby Lane. You'll become part of a community of like-minded artisans, with an audience predisposed towards and interested in the items you've crafted.

SIZE AND TRAFFIC

The only problem with arts and crafts marketplaces is that, with the exception of Etsy, they're not that big. Some of the marketplaces featured in this chapter are quite small indeed, with only a few hundred or thousand sellers, and probably an equal number of regular buyers. That's not a lot of traffic—and the fewer people who see your listings, the fewer potential customers there are.

This argues in favor of picking bigger sites over smaller ones—which typically favors general marketplaces over targeted ones. In other words, eBay is going to put more eyes on your listings than is Funky Finds. There's just no denying that.

The two biggest sites for crafters are eBay and Etsy, although there's an order of magnitude difference between those two. The other sites listed here are considerably smaller than the big two. That doesn't mean they're not worth considering—in fact, some artists and crafters do quite well on the smaller sites—but rather that your upside potential is going to be somewhat limited on those sites.

FEES

A lot of sellers focus on costs rather than potential. That's not the way I do it; sometimes you have to pay more to get a bigger upside. But still, costs are important.

> **TIP** The big sites give you quite a bit extra for the fees you pay. eBay and Etsy, for example, provide a wealth of selling-related services, including payment processing options, as well as increased traffic. In fact, that's one of the reason to pay higher fees—to gain access to a larger potential audience. In a way, the higher fees at a site like eBay are like bundling in your advertising and promotion; you don't have to pay extra to get that exposure to potential customers.

Unfortunately, it's difficult to compare fees from site to site, as everybody does it a little differently. Some charge hefty setup fees; some (most) don't. Some sites charge a monthly fee; some don't. Some charge listing fees; some don't. Some charge selling fees or commissions; some don't.

As such, you kind of have to know how much business and what type of business you'll do before you can compare these apples and oranges. That is, if you have a good idea of how many sales you'll make in a month and the average selling price of your items, you can work through a comparison between sites, using each site's unique fee structure.

Let's say, for example, that you expect to list twenty items and sell ten of them in an average month, at an average selling price of $30. On Etsy, that means you'll pay $4.00 in listing fees and $10.50 in selling fees, for a total cost of $14.50. On eBay, you'll pay $10.00 in listing fees and $33.00 in selling fees, for a total cost of $43.00. On ArtFire, you'd pay a $12.95 monthly subscription fee, but not listing or selling fees, for a total cost of just $12.95.

Of course, there's no guarantee you'd achieve the same level of sales on all three sites. eBay, which looks costly, might be a better deal if you sold twice the number of items as you did on the smaller Etsy site. And ArtFire, which looks darned attractive at first glance, might be a costly bust if you end up selling only one or two items a month.

So you need to consider costs, but also the amount of traffic and potential sales a given site generates. It's not an easy upfront comparison.

> **TIP** I recommend avoiding those sites that charge a hefty setup fee or monthly subscription fees, at least when you're first starting out. You don't want to incur heavy fixed costs until you know for sure whether your crafts will sell and whether a site is worth it.

COMPARING THE BIG TWO: ETSY VS. EBAY

Let's face it. For most crafters, the decision boils down to whether to use Etsy, the largest crafts-only marketplace, or eBay, the largest marketplace period. Both sites can deliver good traffic to your listings and result in decent sales. Which of these sites you choose is as much a philosophical decision as it is a business one.

Despite eBay's higher overall traffic, Etsy may be the more attractive marketplace for those into the handmade culture. Etsy's audience is more targeted, which is nice; you're going to find a pre-qualified, highly receptive audience for your goods on Etsy, as opposed to the more general audience on eBay. And, since Etsy caters to the arts and crafts community, everything tends to "fit" better than it does on the more generic eBay site.

This is especially noticeable in the listings themselves. As you can see in Figures 5.23 and 5.24, Etsy offers much bigger images and more craft-friendly design; eBay's listings are more generic in design, with a lot of extraneous elements that do not enhance the presentation of the craft item for sale. Your crafts simply look better on the Etsy site than on eBay; you also have a more defined individual identity in your listings.

FIGURE 5.23

A craft listing on Etsy—the product really shines.

FIGURE 5.24

A craft listing on eBay—not quite as attractive as the Etsy listing.

Then there are the fees—which are considerably lower on Etsy. For example, Etsy's $0.20 listing fee is less than half that of eBay's $0.50 listing fee for fixed-price (what eBay calls Buy It Now) items. To be fair, the listing fee is only $0.20 if you're listing in an eBay Store, but then you're paying anywhere from $15.95 to $299.95 for your Store subscription, so there's that, too.

The difference in final selling fees is more dramatic. You pay Etsy 3.5% of the final selling price, while you pay eBay a considerably higher 11%. That's noticeable, whether you're selling lower-priced items or higher-priced ones.

eBay also offers the auction option, which Etsy does not. Now, if you know the item you're selling has a fixed value, that doesn't matter—a $20 necklace is worth $20 on either Etsy or eBay, so you might as well sell it at a fixed price. If you're selling rare, collectible, or vintage items, however, the price is more speculative; you may be able to get a higher price by selling it via auction on eBay.

That said, eBay has a much larger potential audience, with more than 200 million registered users vs. Etsy's 12 million or so. This typically results in significantly more traffic for many sellers, even though Etsy's traffic may be more focused. That may mean more potential sales on eBay—or on Etsy. It's hard to tell without trying each out, first.

The decision on which of the two sites to use may also depend, to a degree, on the type of items you're selling. Every category is different. If you're in a more common category, such as vintage clothing or jewelry, eBay may have a lot more traffic than you'll get on Etsy. Less general categories, however, such as handmade bottle stoppers or gourd bottles may have a larger and more receptive audience on Etsy.

At the end of the day, however, the most appealing thing about Etsy for many crafters is that it's a community of arts and crafts lovers. Etsy shoppers value handmade items, and know what to expect; eBay buyers don't always. That makes Etsy a more personal place to do business, which may matter to you. It's a matter of being a bigger fish in a smaller, more cohesive pond versus being a smaller fish in a much larger body of water. There are advantages to both.

SELLING ON YOUR OWN WEBSITE

There's also the option of bypassing third-party marketplaces altogether and launching your own ecommerce website to sell your crafts directly to customers. This option certainly has some appeal, especially if you're moving large quantities of craft items already.

On the plus side, running your own website means you're not obligated to any third party. After you pay your monthly web hosting costs, you don't have to pay anybody else anything (except for payment processing fees, of course); there's no entity to siphon off listing fees and final value fees and commissions and such.

Plus, you get to establish your own identity totally unaffiliated with any other site. Your site is your site, not just a virtual stall in an online marketplace. It's a great branding opportunity.

On the minus side, running your own website is a lot of work. All the design and hosting stuff that an online marketplace does for you, you have to do yourself. That means building the site, maintaining the site, and hosting the site, all of which takes time and costs money. Even though you don't have to pay per-listing or per-sale fees, running your own site is still a costly proposition—and a time consuming one.

It's also a challenge to attract potential customers to your site. When you list on Etsy or eBay or another third-party marketplace, you get to take advantage of their built-in promotion; all the daily visitors they attract are potential customers. When you run your own site, however, nobody knows you're there until you do a bunch of advertising and promotion. You don't have to promote on Etsy or eBay; if you don't spend some bucks to promote your own site, it'll whither on the proverbial vine.

All that said, I wouldn't recommend building your own website if you're just an occasional or growing seller. Full-time sellers, however, need to consider this as an option—not necessarily your only option, but certainly in conjunction with listings on other marketplaces.

> **NOTE** Learn more about building a ecommerce site in Chapter 8, "Selling on Your Own Website."

SETTLING ON A SITE—OR TWO

If you've made it all the way through all the information presented in this chapter—well, good for you! There are a lot of factors you need to consider when choosing where to sell your crafts, and the answers aren't always obvious.

Let's face it, settling on a single site for your crafts is difficult. But there's nothing that says you only have to pick *one* site. Many crafters offer their goods on multiple sites, therefore reaching a larger (and perhaps more diverse) audience than any single site can deliver.

That's right, you can choose to sell on both Etsy and eBay, or on Bonanza and I Made It Myself, or on ShopHandmade and Ruby Lane. You can choose to sell on any or all of the available marketplaces, and on your own site. There are no rules that limit listing your crafts on any single site.

The only limitation, really, is what you have time to manage. Posting listings to multiple sites takes more time than posting to a single site, even if you reuse the product photos and item descriptions. (Which you can and should do, by the way.) It's a matter of uploading listings to each site and then watching and managing those listings on a regular basis.

The more sites you use, the more work you have to do—which argues in favor of keeping to a manageable list of sites. Maybe you use Etsy and eBay and one or two other craft-specific marketplaces and see which of them perform best for you. After a month or two, cut off those sites that aren't working and add one or two new sites to your list. Track sales for another month or two and fine-tune your list further. After six months or so, you'll have a list of sites that you know performs well and are worth the effort.

> **NOTE** Managing your inventory across multiple sites is also somewhat of a challenge; do it wrong, and you could end up selling the same item more than once! Learn more about inventory management—across one site or more—in Chapter 12, "Managing Your Inventory."

Selling on Etsy

6

Etsy is the largest dedicated arts and crafts marketplace on the web. If you're a serious crafter, you're probably already familiar with the site; it's a great place to peruse and buy crafts of all sorts, as well as a good source of craft supplies.

Your challenge now is learning how to use the Etsy site to sell your own handmade crafts. It's actually fairly easy; Etsy provides just about everything you need to get your items listed and (hopefully) selling.

GETTING TO KNOW ETSY

Etsy (www.etsy.com) is a marketplace for artisans and crafters—as the site itself puts it, "your place to buy and sell all things handmade." The site boasts more than 800,000 individual sellers (with more than 7 million items for sale) and more than 12 million buyers. Unlike what seems to be the growing trend on eBay, Etsy sellers are primarily individuals, not retailers.

As to who uses Etsy, it's serious crafters and craft lovers. Etsy users—buyers and sellers alike—tend to be college-educated women in their twenties and thirties. That's one of the things that makes Etsy an attractive marketplace for craft-related sellers.

> **TIP** In addition to being a great place to sell your completed crafts, Etsy is also a good site to purchase your craft supplies. In fact, some of Etsy's largest sellers are craft suppliers, selling things like beads, candle scents, and the like.

Figure 6.1 shows the Etsy home page. Shoppers can browse for items by category or search for specific items using the top-of-page search box. The home page displays a variety of items handpicked by a chosen user; these items vary from day to day. The site also hosts a vibrant user community, in the form of a pretty decent company blog and a set of well-trafficked user forums.

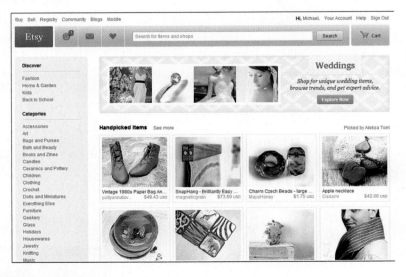

FIGURE 6.1

The Etsy home page; navigate from the categories at the left or search for items using the top-of-page search box.

WHAT CAN YOU SELL ON ETSY?

As befits its reputation as a marketplace for handmade crafts, Etsy tends to be a site for lower-priced items, in general. The average sale runs in the $15 to $20 range, although higher-priced items (especially vintage items) can be found.

Anything you sell on Etsy either has to be either handmade, vintage (more than 20 years old), or a supply. You can list items in a variety of popular crafts categories, including the following:

- Accessories
- Art
- Bags and Purses
- Bath and Beauty
- Books and Zines
- Candles
- Ceramics and Pottery
- Children
- Clothing
- Crochet
- Dolls and Miniatures
- Everything Else
- Furniture
- Geekery
- Glass
- Holidays
- Housewares
- Jewelry
- Knitting
- Music
- Needlecraft
- Paper Goods
- Patterns
- Pets
- Plants and Edibles
- Quilts
- Supplies
- Toys
- Vintage
- Weddings
- Woodworking

You should be able to fit your crafts into one of these categories, and their associated subcategories. For example, the Candles category includes subcategories for Beeswax, Container, Holder, Incense, Pillar, Scented, Shaped, Soy, Taper, Tart, Tea Light, Tin, Travel, Unscented, Vegan, and Votive candles. There are even subcategories within subcategories; for example, the Tea Light subcategory includes further subcategories for Beeswax, Scented, Soy, Sweet, Unscented, Vegan, and White. (Figure 6.2 shows the various Candles subcategories.) So if you sell scented tea light candles, you'd list your items under **Candles > Tea Light > Scented**.

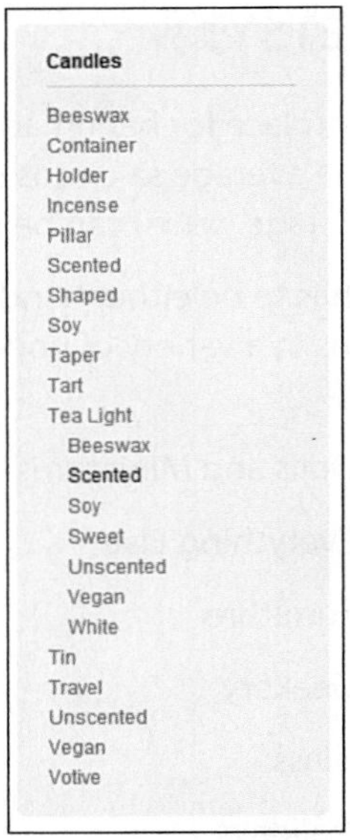

Candles

Beeswax
Container
Holder
Incense
Pillar
Scented
Shaped
Soy
Taper
Tart
Tea Light
   Beeswax
   Scented
   Soy
   Sweet
   Unscented
   Vegan
   White
Tin
Travel
Unscented
Vegan
Votive

FIGURE 6.2

Viewing the various subcategories in Etsy's Candles category.

NOTE Etsy is an equal-opportunity craft marketplace, but some things do sell better than others. The top ten craft categories on Etsy are, in order, Jewelry, Accessories, Housewares, Clothing, Bags and Purses, Crochet, Knitting, Glass, Ceramics and Pottery, and Dolls and Miniatures.

HOW DOES ETSY WORK?

Before you sell on Etsy, you create your own Etsy shop. This is your personal presence on the Etsy site, home to all the items you choose to sell. Each Etsy shop has its unique web address (URL), in the form of www.etsy.com/shop/*storename*.

As you can see in Figure 6.3, a typical Etsy shop includes a cover image at the top, accompanied by a short description, followed by all the items listed by the store owner. Contact information and such for the seller is displayed in the left column.

You then create detailed listings for the items you want to sell. A typical Etsy item listing, like the one in Figure 6.4, includes one or more photos of an item, along with a detailed text description. Information about the seller is in the right column, along with the item price and a big green Add to Cart button.

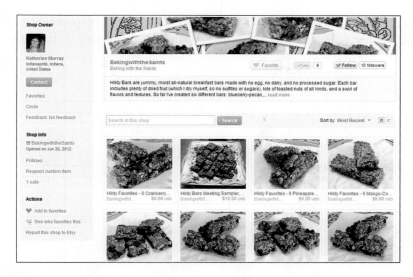

FIGURE 6.3

A typical Etsy shop—BakingwiththeSaints from seller Katherine Murray (www.etsy.com/shop/ BakingwiththeSaints).

FIGURE 6.4

A typical Etsy listing, for a hairbow set from seller Susan Looney's BOWZETC shop (www.etsy.com/ shop/BOWZETC).

Beneath the item listing proper is information about shipping and payment methods, as shown in Figure 6.5. There's also a selection of similar items offered by the same seller.

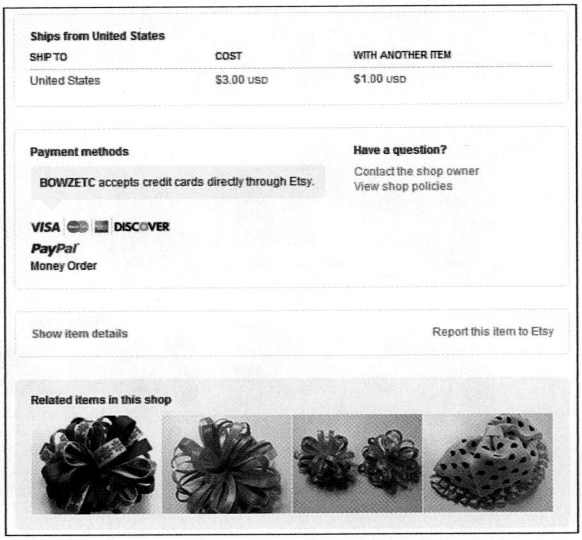

FIGURE 6.5
Shipping and payment information, along with similar items for sale, beneath an item listing.

For customers, purchasing an item is as easy as clicking the green Add to Cart button. Unlike most other online marketplaces, Etsy enables customers to purchase from multiple sellers and then check out through a single process. Etsy offers multiple payment methods, including credit cards, money orders, and the ubiquitous PayPal.

WHAT IT COSTS TO SELL ON ETSY

Etsy costs a little more to use than smaller craft-focused sites, but less than the larger eBay, which does not have a craft focus. All the fees are paid by sellers; buyers don't have to pay any fees to Etsy.

NOTE Etsy also offers you the opportunity to advertise your shop and listings, in the form of search advertising, for an additional cost. Learn more at www.etsy.com/search-ads/.

ETSY SHOP FEES

Let's start with what it costs to set up an Etsy shop. That cost is easy to calculate—it's zero. That's right, your Etsy store is free, both to set up and maintain on a month-to-month basis. (Compare that to an eBay Store, which costs a minimum of $15.95 per month.)

LISTING FEES

Next up are listing fees. A listing fee is what you pay when you first list an item for sale, and on Etsy, it's $0.20. That is, you pay $0.20 for each item you have for sale. For example, if you have three different types of gift baskets to sell, you pay $0.20 for each listing, for a total of $0.60.

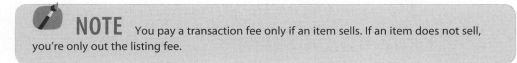

NOTE You pay the initial listing fee whether an item sells or not. The fee is for the listing, not for the sale.

If you have more than one of a given item to sell, the listing fee is still $0.20—sort of. When you sell one of the items from a multiple-quantity listing, Etsy automatically renews the listing for a new $0.20 listing fee. And if you sell more than one of an item to a single customer, you're charged a "multiple quantity fee" of $0.20 for each item sold (after the first) in that transaction. The practical effect is that you pay $0.20 for each item you have for sale, whether it's upfront or when the item is sold.

Each listing is good for four months, or until you cancel it, whichever comes first. If you want to renew a listing for another four months, you pay the $0.20 listing fee again. You'll also need to pay another $0.20 if you want to relist an item that has sold.

TRANSACTION FEES

When you sell an item, you pay Etsy a 3.5% transaction fee. This fee is calculated on the final selling price, not including tax or shipping fees. So if you sell an item for $20, you pay 3.5% of that $20, or $0.70.

NOTE You pay a transaction fee only if an item sells. If an item does not sell, you're only out the listing fee.

PAYMENT PROCESSING FEES

If you use Etsy's direct checkout system for your shop (more on this later in the chapter), Etsy handles your payment processing—for a fee. Etsy's payment processing fee is 3% of the total amount paid (including tax and shipping fees), plus a flat $0.25 per order.

For example, let's say you sell an item for $20 plus $5 shipping/handling, no tax collected. You'd pay 3% of the total $25 (that's $0.75), plus the $0.25 flat fee, for a total of $1.00 in payment processing fees.

PAYING ETSY

Listing, transaction, and advertising fees are billed once a month. Your Etsy bill is due by the 15th of each month, and can be paid via your PayPal account or a credit card you leave on file with the site.

Payment processing fees, on the other hand, are deducted from the transaction amount when Etsy deposits those funds in your account. So if you owe $1 worth of payment processing fees on a $25 (total) transaction, Etsy only deposits the net $24 in your account.

SIGNING UP FOR AN ETSY ACCOUNT

To sell on Etsy, you have to register for an account. There are actually two ways to do this.

The first method is easiest if you already have a Facebook account and don't mind linking it with your new Etsy account. Just go to the Etsy home page (www.etsy.com) and click Register in the top of page toolbar. When the next page appears, as shown in Figure 6.6, click the Sign Up Using Facebook button. If you're already logged into Facebook, you'll be prompted for your permission to link the accounts, as shown in Figure 6.7; click Add to Facebook and you're signed up. (If you're not currently logged into Facebook, you'll first be prompted to enter your Facebook username and password.)

FIGURE 6.6

Signing up for Etsy with your Facebook account.

FIGURE 6.7

Giving your permission to link your Etsy and Facebook accounts.

If you're not a Facebook member, or prefer not to link to your Facebook account, you can sign up using your email address. As you can see in Figure 6.8, enter your first and last name, gender, email address, desired password, and desired username, and then click the Register button. Etsy then sends you a confirmation email; click the link there and you're in.

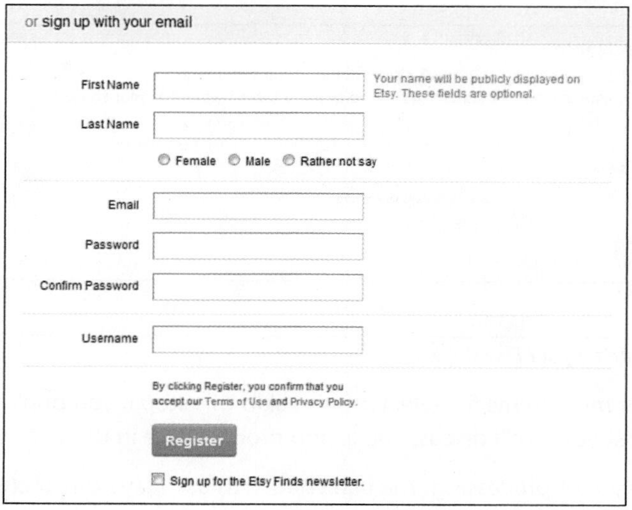

FIGURE 6.8

Signing up for Etsy with your email account.

SETTING UP YOUR ETSY SHOP

Before you can start selling on Etsy, you have to create your own personal Etsy shop. This is essentially your online storefront on the Etsy site, where all the listings you post of items for sale are displayed.

CREATING YOUR SHOP

To create your Etsy shop, start by clicking the Sell link at the top of the Etsy home page. When the next page appears, click the Open an Etsy Shop button.

You're now prompted to set up the language, currency, and region for your shop. If you're in the U.S., Etsy suggests the English language, U.S. dollar, and the United States; click Yes to accept these.

Etsy now leads you through the four steps of creating your shop:

1. Enter the desired name for your shop, as shown in Figure 6.9. Your shop name should reflect the types of items you sell, or any identity you've previously established (for example, if you have a similar storefront on another site, or in the real world).

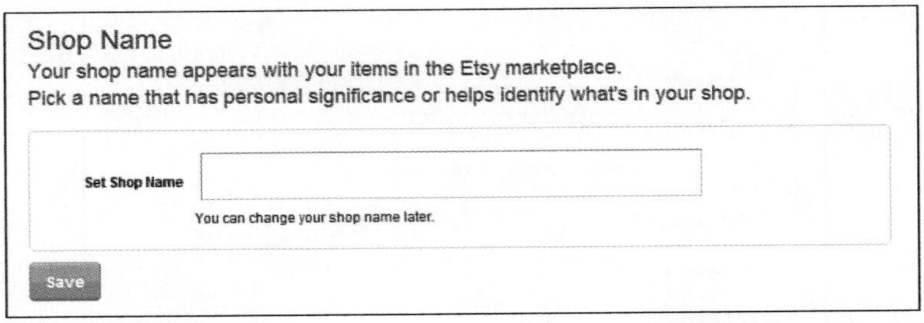

Shop Name
Your shop name appears with your items in the Etsy marketplace.
Pick a name that has personal significance or helps identify what's in your shop.

Set Shop Name [   ]

You can change your shop name later.

[Save]

FIGURE 6.9
Entering a name for your Etsy shop.

2. List one or more items for sale. (You can skip this step if you don't have anything ready to list yet.) We'll discuss the listing process later in this chapter.

3. Set up payment processing. You can choose to use Etsy's direct checkout system, or select other payment methods. We'll discuss this later in the chapter, as well.

4. Arrange payment for your Etsy fees. You have to give Etsy your credit card number so that your card can be charged for the fees you incur each month.

CUSTOMIZING YOUR SHOP

That's the initial stuff. Past that, you can customize your shop with any or all of the following items:

- Top-of-page banner image.
- Shop title.
- Shop announcement (text about your shop that all shoppers see).
- Links to your Facebook and Twitter accounts, so shoppers can "like" and tweet about your shop.
- Sections for different types of merchandise. (For example, if you sell candles, you can include individual sections of your shop for different types of candles, or different scents or colors.)
- Personal information in your Etsy profile.
- Your personal profile picture.
- Your location.
- Shop policies, such as your payment policy, shipping policy, and refund policy.

You enter all these items from your main shop page, which you display by clicking the name of your shop at the top of the Etsy home page. What you see here is the basic template of your shop page, as shown in Figure 6.10. Click any section to edit that section.

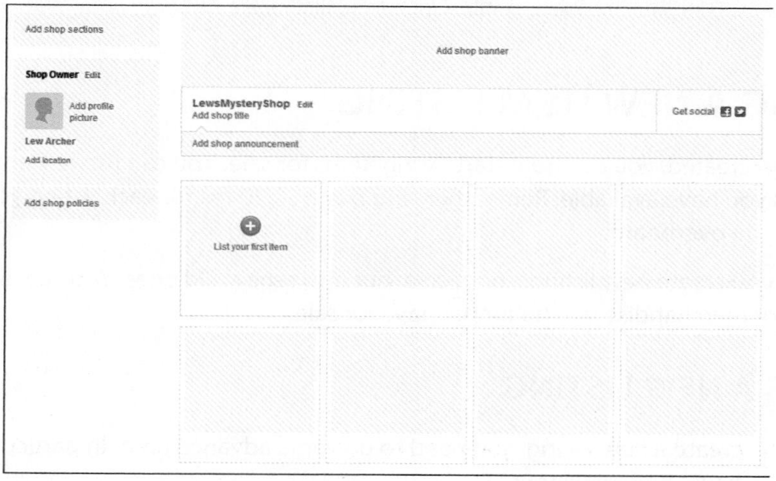

FIGURE 6.10

Editing sections of your Etsy shop page.

For example, to enter your shop policies, click Add Shop Policies. This displays the Shop Policies page, shown in Figure 6.11. Enter your policies into the appropriate boxes; then click the Save button when done. Other sections of your shop page are edited in the same fashion.

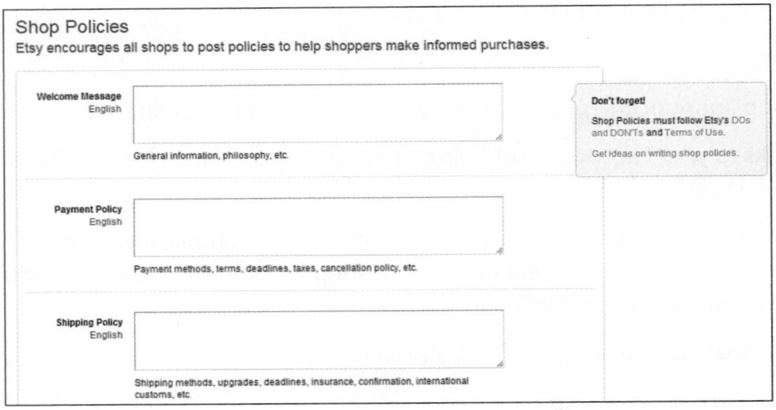

FIGURE 6.11

Entering your shop policies.

> ✂ **TIP**   You can also edit your personal information by mousing over Your Account at the top of any Etsy page and selecting Public Profile.

CREATING A NEW ITEM LISTING

Your shop created, you can now start listing items for sale. You can list as many items as you like or as you have available. Remember, you pay a $0.20 fee for each listing you create, so don't go too overboard.

Etsy lets you create new listings, of course, but also renew old ones. You can also "deactivate" listings for merchandise you no longer have for sale.

STARTING A NEW LISTING

Before you create a new listing, you need to do some advance prep. In particular, you need to know or have the following:

- One or more digital photos of the item
- The item's title and description

■ Necessary information for the item's shipping description

■ Which category you want to place the item in

With that information at hand, you get started by following these general steps:

1. Click Sell at the top of any Etsy page.

2. When the Sell on Etsy page appears, click the List an Item button.

3. When the List an Item page appears, as shown in Figure 6.12, fill in all the necessary information. This include who made the item, the listing category, item title, and description.

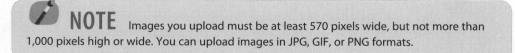

List an Item

About this Item — Who made it?
Select a maker...

Categories — What is it?
Select a category...

Photos
⊕
ADD PHOTOS
Convey the shape, size, color, and texture. Try to use natural light and include a great close up.

Great Product Photos
Watch the Video

Item Title
Descriptive titles are best. Try to describe your item the way a shopper would.

Description
Try to answer the questions shoppers will have. Tell the item's story and explain why it's special.

FIGURE 6.12

Creating a new item listing.

4. To upload photos of the item, click Add Photos and select up to five images to include in your listing.

> ✎ **NOTE** Images you upload must be at least 570 pixels wide, but not more than 1,000 pixels high or wide. You can upload images in JPG, GIF, or PNG formats.

5. Fill in all optional information, including which section of your shop the item belongs in (if your shop has multiple sections), who the item is made for (recipient), what special event the item is for (occasion), and what style the item is.

6. Enter up to 13 tags that describe your item.

NOTE A tag is a keyword or phrase that someone might use to search for your item. Selecting the right tags helps your item appear higher on results pages when someone is searching for a similar item.

7. Enter the materials used to construct your item. (You can enter up to 13 materials.)
8. Enter the item's selling price into the Price box.
9. Enter how many of this particular item you have for sale into the Quantity box.
10. Enter the appropriate shipping information into the Shipping section, shown in Figure 6.13—your shipping location, shipping fees, and so forth.

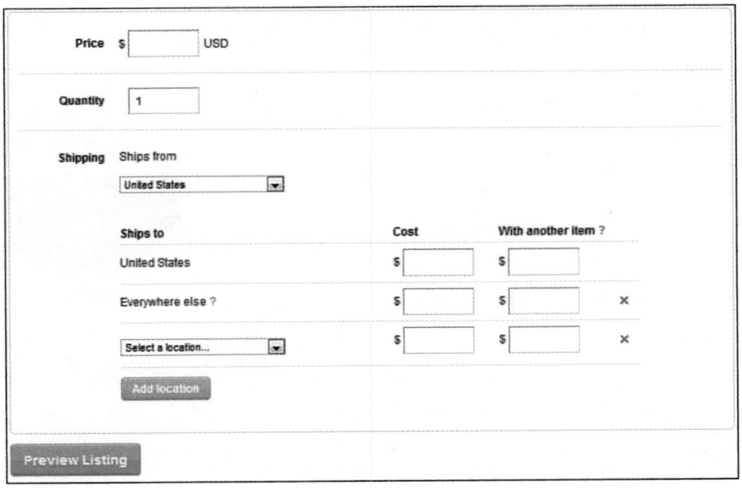

FIGURE 6.13
Entering shipping information.

TIP The shipping fees you charge should include actual shipping, the cost of packing materials, and any reasonable "handling charges" to compensate you for your time.

11. Click the Preview Listing button to see what your listing looks like.
12. If you like what you see, click the Publish button.

Your listing is now submitted to Etsy and appears in your Etsy shop and in Etsy's category and search listings.

EDITING AN ITEM LISTING

What do you do if you didn't quite get an item listing right, or later decide you need to change some of the details? Fortunately, Etsy lets you easily edit any existing item listing.

To edit a listing, click the name of your shop at the top of any Etsy page to open your Etsy shop; click the listing you want to edit. When the listing opens, click the Edit link in the Listing Tools toolbar at the top of the listing. This displays the Edit Listing page; edit the section or sections you want, and then click the Preview Listing button to preview your changes. Click the Publish button to make your changes permanent.

RENEWING A LISTING

An Etsy listing is good for four months, or until an item sells, whichever comes first. When an item sells, you can renew the listing with fresh merchandise; you can also renew expired listings.

To renew a listing, click Your Account at the top of any Etsy page; when the Your Account page opens, click Sold Orders (in the Orders section) on the left side of the page. When the Orders page opens, click the All tab and click the Renew Sold link for the item you wish to renew. When the Edit Listing page appears, change any information as necessary, and then click the Renew button.

DEACTIVATING A LISTING

Sometimes you decide not to sell an item that you've already listed. Or maybe you have an item listed on Etsy and another site, and you sell the item from that other site. Whatever the reason, Etsy lets you cancel or "deactivate" any active listing.

To deactivate a listing, click Your Account at the top of any Etsy page, and then click Listings. Go to the Active section and check the item you wish to remove. Click the Deactivate button, and that item is removed from your active listings.

GETTING PAID

Etsy offers various ways for customers to pay for their purchases—and for sellers to get paid. The default method is Etsy's direct checkout system, but you can also choose to accept payments via PayPal, money order, or personal check.

> **NOTE** Learn more about various payment methods in Chapter 9, "Handling Online Payments."

You select your payment method by clicking Your Shop at the top of any Etsy page, and then clicking Shipping & Payment. Go to the Payment Methods section and select Etsy's direct payment or other payment methods.

The reality is that the vast majority of online shoppers, at Etsy or elsewhere, prefer to pay via credit card. Given that you're probably not set up as a credit card merchant, you can use either Etsy's direct checkout system to handle credit card processing. We'll look at each separately.

ETSY DIRECT CHECKOUT

Etsy's direct checkout system is a payment processing system, much like PayPal, that enables sellers to accept customers' credit card payments. The customer pays Etsy via the direct checkout system, Etsy handles all the credit card processing operations, and then Etsy deposits the funds into the seller's account.

One of the nice things about direct checkout is that all payment operations are handled on the Etsy site; the customer doesn't have to be directed to another site to pay for an item, as is the case with PayPal payments. In addition, customers paying via direct checkout can purchase items from multiple sellers and check out in a single process.

As with any payment processing system, there are fees incurred for using the direct checkout system. (Fees for the seller, that is; the buyer doesn't pay any additional fees.) You pay $0.25 per transaction, plus 3% of the total payment. That total includes any tax and shipping fees paid by the customer.

As an example, envision the sale of a $20 item with a $5 shipping charge. That's a $25 total transaction value, of which you pay 3%, or $0.75, plus the flat $0.25 fee. That's a total of $1.00, then, in payment processing fees charged.

NOTE Etsy will electronically deposit funds due from a sale into your designated bank account once you mark the item "shipped." It typically takes three days for funds to be available in your account.

PAYPAL

You can also opt to use PayPal for your payment processing for Etsy sales. PayPal is well known by shoppers across the web; many online retailers use PayPal for their payment processing.

If you choose to accept PayPal payments instead of or in addition to Etsy's direct checkout, you'll need to first establish your own PayPal account, and then enter the email address

associated with that account when you choose your Etsy payment methods. The PayPal option then appears when a customer purchases an item from your shop, and PayPal handles all the credit card processing and deposits the appropriate funds into your checking account.

PayPal's fees are similar to those of Etsy's direct checkout system, although calculated a little differently. PayPal charges sellers a flat $0.30 per transaction (Etsy charges $0.25), plus 2.9% of the transaction value (Etsy charges 3%). For most sellers, that figures out pretty close. It's really a matter of which payment processing service you prefer, as well as which you think your customers will like best.

OTHER PAYMENT METHODS

Etsy also lets you accept payment via money order or personal check. In both instances, that means that the buyer sends you a check in the mail. You wait for the check to arrive, and then deposit it. In the case of a money order, it should be good as soon as deposited. In the case of a personal check, you better hold it for two weeks or so to make sure it clears, before you ship the item.

TIP Few online sellers these days accept payment via check or money order, and few buyers pay this way. Most buyers pay via credit card, which necessitates the use of Etsy's direct checkout or PayPal—and means you get paid when the sale is made, not days or weeks after.

MANAGING YOUR ETSY SALES

Managing your Etsy listings and sales on an ongoing basis is fairly routine.

When a customer buys an item from your shop, Etsy notifies you via email. If the payment was via PayPal or Etsy's direct checkout, you can immediately ship the item to the seller. If payment was via check or money order, you'll need to wait for the payment to arrive in the mail, and then ship the item. (In the case of payment via personal check, wait until the check clears before you ship.) You then have the option of relisting that item, if you have another to sell.

TIP You can keep track of all your sales from your Your Account page, which you access by clicking Your Account at the top of any Etsy page. To view your sales, click Sold Orders (in the Orders section) on the left side of the page.

If an item goes unsold for four months, the item listing expires. You then have the option of renewing the listing (for another $0.20) or just moving on.

TIPS FOR MAKING MORE MONEY ON ETSY

Now, don't expect to list a dozen items on Etsy and immediately be notified of sales for each item. Things don't happen that fast, at least not normally. Any given item may be listed for a month or more before it sells; some items may never sell. That's just the way things work.

With that in mind, there are some things you can do to maximize your Etsy sales and profits. Let's take a look at some useful tips.

SPRUCE UP YOUR SHOP

One Etsy shop looks just like the others—unless you personalize it. That means adding a distinctive cover image, unique descriptive text, and a useful and appealing profile picture.

CREATE A POWERFUL COVER IMAGE

People buy with their eyes. That argues for including multiple attractive product photos, of course, but also in adding an appealing cover image at the top of your shop page. That cover image is the first thing most shoppers will see; you want that image to grab potential customers and sell them on your shop.

What kinds of cover image should you create? There are lots of ways to go:

- Incorporate your name or logo into the image, as shown in Figure 6.14.

- Show samples of your products in the image, as shown in Figure 6.15.

- Use the image as a banner ad to announce your current promotion, as shown in Figure 6.16.

I also like cover images with people in them, like the one in Figure 6.17; human faces (especially the eyes) help to draw visitors into the page.

FIGURE 6.14

A cover image of the shop's name. (Courtesy PimentoCheeseVintage.)

FIGURE 6.15

A cover image with photos of the seller's crafts. (Courtesy eric8429, ShineDIY.)

FIGURE 6.16

A cover image as banner advertisement. (Courtesy shareliving, Jewelry Findings Supplies.)

FIGURE 6.17

A cover image with a human touch. (Courtesy iheartnorwegianwood.)

TIP Creating an attractive cover image typically involves a bit of photography, some work in Photoshop or another image editing program, and some real honest to goodness graphic design. If that's not your forte, farm it out to a professional designer; it's worth the expense.

LIST MORE TO SELL MORE

To some degree, selling your crafts on Etsy is a numbers game. If you only have one item for sale, you probably won't sell as much than if you have two or three or more items for sale. The more items available, the more likely it is that a customer will find something worth buying.

In addition, an Etsy shop with only a few items listed looks bare; it looks as if the seller really isn't into it. On the other hand, a shop with lots of items for sale looks like a serious business, with lots of interesting items for customers to browse. The more items you can list and display, the better.

LIST OR RENEW DAILY

One way to attract customers to your store is to always have new merchandise available. New listings also help your store in the search results. To that end, list or renew at least one item each day. It's worth the $0.20.

MAKE SURE YOU TAG YOUR ITEMS

I mentioned this briefly when discussing how to create an item listing, but it's very important that you "tag" the items you list for sale. Tags are how potential customers find your items when they're searching for something to buy. You can add up to 13 tags, and you should use every available slot.

Use tags that describe your item and that match the terms people use when searching. For example, if you're selling handmade vanilla scented tea light candles, you can use tags such as **vanilla candle**, **vanilla tea candle**, **tea light candle**, **scented tea candle**, **handmade candle**, **small candle**, **white candle**, and so forth—any possible way that customers might describe the item.

> **TIP** Tagged items not only appear in Etsy search results, but can also appear in Google search results when users are using that popular search site.

PACK PROMOTIONALLY

When you pack the items you sell, use this opportunity to promote your Etsy shop and other items you have for sale. That might mean including a business card, promotional brochure, or even just a sheet of paper listing other items you currently have for sale. And make sure your packaging is professional; you don't want to turn off repeat buyers with a shabby box job.

INCREASE YOUR FEEDBACK BY BUYING ON ETSY

Customers look to a seller's feedback rating to determine the reliability of that seller. If you're a new seller without a lot of sales under your belt (and thus a low feedback rating), you can increase your rating by making purchases from other Etsy sellers. They'll leave you positive feedback, and that ups your rating. In particular, consider buying your craft supplies on Etsy; you need those supplies anyway, so why not buy from fellow Etsy merchants and increase your feedback, to boot?

Selling on eBay

7

Etsy is the largest crafts-specific marketplace on the Internet, but it pales in size in comparison to eBay, which is the largest online marketplace, period. If you want the largest possible audience for the crafts you sell, eBay is the place to be.

UNDERSTANDING EBAY

What is eBay? As you can see in Figure 7.1, it's an online marketplace, with categories for all sorts of items. I could describe the site in more detail, but the best description comes from eBay itself:

> eBay is the world's largest online marketplace, where practically anyone can buy and sell practically anything.

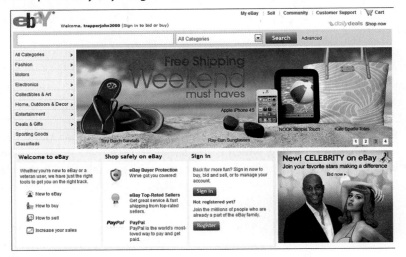

FIGURE 7.1
eBay—the world's largest online marketplace.

Note that phrase, "practically anything." Unlike Etsy, eBay isn't just for arts and crafts; you can sell just about anything you imagine in the eBay marketplace, from antiques and automobiles to video games and vintage clothing, and everything in between—including arts and crafts items.

SIZE MATTERS

Just how big is eBay? Look at these statistics:

- On any given day, eBay has more than 100 million items listed for sale.
- As of the end of 2011, eBay had more than 100 million active users worldwide.
- During the entire year of 2011, $68.6 billion worth of merchandise was traded over eBay—almost $2,100 per second.

All this activity makes eBay not only the biggest shopping site on the Internet, but one of the largest online communities of any type.

WHO SELLS ON EBAY?

So, who's selling all the merchandise listed on the eBay site? There's not a simple answer to that question; there are tens of millions of sellers, representing a broad variety of people and businesses. It's not just crafters, that's for sure.

The first group of eBay sellers are just regular people, not professional sellers. They're not businesses, and they're not trying to make a living from it; they're just selling stuff they don't want anymore. To them, eBay is the 21st-century equivalent of a garage sale.

Next are those individuals who *are* trying to make a living from their eBay sales. These are crafters selling their wares online, or people who purchase merchandise specifically for resale. Some of these sellers are successful, some aren't; that's the way the world works.

Finally, we have a variety of companies that sell on eBay. These may be businesses that exist online only, or traditional brick-and-mortar businesses who also sell online. These sellers are very professional, and often have their own eBay Stores.

EBAY FOR CRAFTERS

Even though eBay isn't focused solely on artists and crafters, it is a large marketplace for arts and crafts. Not every crafter likes eBay, although a lot do.

If you create your own artwork or crafts, what benefits do you get by selling your work on eBay? The primary benefit, of course, is traffic—of which there's a lot more of it than with any other online marketplace. With 100 million registered users, eBay provides access to a lot of potential customers for your crafts. No other site comes close in terms of traffic; if you want to go where the customers are, eBay's the place.

That said, eBay isn't all cookies and cream for the craft world, primarily because all that traffic isn't there for the arts and crafts. A huge hunk of eBay's potential buyers are there to buy something else, and are looking for bargains. Yes, you can get a lot of lookers for your crafts, but they may not be particularly craft savvy.

The fact that eBay is a mass market, not a specialized one, can result in a few issues. It's a sad fact that eBay's audience does not include a lot of die-hard craft arts and crafts lovers. Because of that, highly stylized, "arty" work doesn't always sell that well; paintings of cute cats and dogs do. Depending on your style and sensibility, this may not be the best venue for the types of crafts you create.

In addition, you may be disappointed in the selling prices on eBay, especially for auction-style listings; artwork and handmade crafts don't always command high prices at auction. Original art goes for more than prints, but it's still a buyer's market. eBay tends to be more for bargain hunters than art lovers, so reaching a sufficient volume of work will be important.

For artists and crafters, these are the realities you have to face up to when selling on eBay. It may be a good deal, or it may not. Your mileage will vary.

HOW TO SELL ON EBAY

eBay started out as a pure online auction site; every transaction was conducted via the online auction format. While about half of eBay's sales still come from online auctions, a growing percentage of transactions come from fixed-price listings. In reality, there are four different ways to sell on eBay, and not all are equally suited for crafters.

AUCTION LISTINGS

For many years, the only way to sell on eBay was via online auction. That's changed, of course, but the auction format is still preferred by a surprising number of buyers and sellers. Buyers like it because it provides significant upside if the price of an item gets bid up; sellers like it for the converse reason, that they sometimes get a bargain if there's little bidding on an item. (Figure 7.2 shows a typical auction listing, note the Starting Bid price and Place Bid button.)

FIGURE 7.2

A typical auction-style listing on the eBay site.

First off, it helps to understand exactly what an eBay auction is and how it works. If you've never used eBay before, you might be a little anxious about what might be involved. But don't fret; an eBay auction is really just an Internet-based version of a traditional auction—you know, the type where a fast-talking auctioneer stands in the front of the room, trying to coax potential buyers into bidding just a little bit more for the piece of merchandise up for bid. The only difference is that there's no fast-talking auctioneer online (the bidding process is executed by special auction software on the auction site), and all the bidders aren't in the same room.

The process starts when you, the seller, create an item listing on the eBay site. You specify the length of the auction (1, 3, 5, 7, or 10 days) and the minimum bid you will accept for that item. That's where the bidding starts. (It's also where your fees start; eBay charges a flat fee for each listing you create.)

A potential buyer searching for a particular type of item (or just browsing through all the merchandise listed in a specific category) reads the item listing and decides to make a bid. The bidder specifies the maximum amount he or she will pay; this amount has to be equal to or greater than the seller's minimum required bid, or higher than any other existing bids.

eBay's built-in bidding software automatically places a bid for the bidder that bests the current bid by a specified amount—but doesn't reveal the bidder's maximum bid. For example, the current bid on an item might be $10. A bidder is willing to pay up to $20 for the item, and thus enters a maximum bid of $20. eBay's "proxy" software places a bid for the new bidder in the amount of $11—higher than the current bid, but less than the specified maximum bid. If there are no other bids, this bidder will win the auction with a $11 bid. Other potential buyers, however, can place additional bids; unless their maximum bids are more than the current bidder's $20 maximum, they are informed (by email) that they have been outbid—and the first bidder's current bid is automatically raised to match the new bids (up to the specified maximum bid price).

At the conclusion of an auction, eBay informs the high bidder of his or her winning bid, and the buyer arranges payment, typically via PayPal. You, the seller, are notified of the winning bid and payment, and then pack and ship the item to the winning bidder. eBay bills you a percentage of the final bid price as a selling fee, and the transaction is concluded.

> **NOTE** Learn more about eBay auctions in my companion book, *Sams Teach Yourself eBay in 10 Minutes* (Sams, 2011), available in bookstores everywhere.

AUCTIONS WITH THE BUY IT NOW OPTION

eBay has a variation on the traditional auction format called the Buy It Now (BIN) option. This is essentially a fixed price alternative to bidding; when a seller establishes a BIN price for an item, in addition to the normal auction starting price), a buyer can end the auction early by paying the fixed price. (Figure 7.3 shows an auction listing with the Buy It Now option.)

FIGURE 7.3

An auction listing with the Buy It Now option.

For example, let's say you list an item with a $10 minimum bid price. You'd be happy if the item sold for $20, you're not so greedy that you want to wait for bidding to take the price higher, so you set a BIN price of $20. If a person perusing your listing thinks that $20 is a fair price, she clicks the Buy It Now button and ends the auction at a $20 selling price.

FIXED PRICE LISTINGS

eBay also offers plain old fixed price listings. These are like auction listings, but the item is offered only at a set price, there's no bidding involved. (Figure 7.4 shows a typical fixed price listing; note the lack of a bidding option, and the Buy It Now button.)

When someone opts to buy the item, she does, for the price listed. There's also a difference in duration; fixed-price listing can be either for 1, 3, 5, 7, or 10 days, like the auction format, but can also run 30 days or what eBay calls Good 'Til Cancelled.

FIGURE 7.4

A fixed-price listing; no bidding option available.

EBAY STORE LISTINGS

Then we have eBay Stores—your own personal storefront on the eBay site. An eBay Store is much like an Etsy Shop, in that it's where you park all the items you have for sale, for an extended period of time. Listing fees are lower for eBay Store items ($0.20 vs. $0.50 for other types of listings). A Store listing is a fixed price listing, but with the lower insertion fee.

Not surprisingly, you have to pay extra to create and maintain an eBay Store. Monthly fees start at $15.95 and go higher, depending on what features you want or need.

WHICH TYPE OF LISTING IS BEST FOR YOU?

The first choice you have to make is whether to go with an auction or fixed price listing. For most handmade craft items, fixed price is probably the way to go.

You see, auctions are great for items where you're not quite sure of the value. You set a reasonable minimum bid price and then let the market (in the form of interested bidders) do its thing. If enough people think an item is worth enough, the bidding process takes the price to an acceptable level. If potential buyers, on the other hand, either aren't that interested or don't place that high a value on an item, the price doesn't get bid up that much.

The thing is, most craft items have a distinct value. If you're selling a handmade bow that most crafters sell for around $10, there's not much point putting it up for auction in the hopes of someone bidding the price up to $20. It's a $10 item, so you might as well list it for that.

In addition, fixed-price listings let you keep your item on the eBay site longer. The longest you can list an item in the auction format is 10 days; with a fixed price listing, you can list for 30 days or until you cancel the listing. That's more the nature of craft selling, where you shouldn't get your hopes up for selling every item you create—at least not immediately. While some artists and crafters achieve high sell-through rates, others sell only about 20% of what they list. It's important to use the longer 30-day fixed price listings and then relist your unsold items and perhaps establish an eBay Store to "park" your previously listed items. In this instance, your eBay Store becomes a virtual gallery for your work.

An eBay Store is also a good idea if you have a lot of lower-priced items to sell—especially pieces that might serve as "accessories" to other items. Sometimes a buyer will like your work but not want to splurge for a high-priced piece; having some smaller (and lower-priced) alternatives available in the Store might salvage a sale. And you can often make profitable add-on sales when a customer finds something else they like in your Store.

UNDERSTANDING EBAY'S FEES

As can be expected, it's not free to sell on eBay. In fact, eBay has a very complicated and somewhat confusing fee structure.

It seems simple enough at first glance. Like Etsy, eBay charges two main types of fees:

- Insertion (listing) fees are what you pay every time you list an item for sale. These fees are based on the minimum bid or fixed price, and are nonrefundable.

- Final value (selling) fees are what you pay when an item is actually sold to a buyer. These fees are based on the item's final selling price (the highest bid). If your item doesn't sell, you aren't charged a final value fee.

eBay also charges various fees for different types of listing enhancements, such as subtitles and fancy listing themes. And if you have an eBay Store, there are monthly subscription fees for that, which we'll discuss later in this chapter

Table 7.1 lists all of eBay's listing fees, current as of August, 2012. Note that many of these fees differ by product category. (I haven't included fees for items listed on the eBay Real Estate and eBay Motors sites; they're typically higher.)

Table 7.1	eBay Fees	
Type of Fee	**Explanation**	**Fee**
Insertion fee (auctions)	In a regular auction, based on the opening bid amount. In a Reserve price auction, based on the reserve price. First 50 auction-style listings each month are free.	Items priced $0.01–$0.99: $0.10 Items priced $1.00–$9.99: $0.25 Items priced $10.00–$24.99: $0.50 Items priced $25.00–$49.99: $0.75 Items priced $50.00–$199.99: $1.00 Items priced $200.00 or more: $2.00
Insertion fee (fixed-price listing)	Items must have a listing price of at least $0.99.	$0.50
Insertion fee (fixed-price listing in eBay Store)	Fees based on subscription level.	$0.20 (Basic), $0.05 (Premium), $0.02 (Anchor)
Final value fee (auctions)	Based on the closing bid.	9.0% of sale price (maximum charge $250.00)
Final value fee (fixed-price listing: electronics)	Based on final selling price.	Items sold for $0.99–$50.00: 7.0% Items sold for $50.01–$1,000.00: 7.0% of initial $50.00, plus 5.0% of remaining sale price Items sold for $1,000.01 or more: 7.0% of initial $50.00, plus 5.0% of next $50.01–$1,000.00, plus 2.0% of remaining sale price
Final value fee (fixed-price listing: clothing, shoes, and accessories)	Based on final selling price.	Items sold for $0.99–$50.00: 10.0% Items sold for $50.01–$1,000.00: 10.0% of initial $50.00, plus 8.0% of remaining sale price Items sold for $1,000.01 or more: 10.0% of initial $50.00, plus 8.0% of next $50.01–$1,000.00, plus 2.0% of remaining sale price

Type of Fee	Explanation	Fee
Final value fee (fixed-price listing: books, DVDs & movies, music, video games)	Based on final selling price.	Items sold for $0.99–$50.00: 13.0% Items sold for $50.01–$1,000.00: 13.0% of initial $50.00, plus 5.0% of remaining sale price Items sold for $1,000.01 or more: 13.0% of initial $50.00, plus 5.0% of next $50.01–$1,000.00, plus 2.0% of remaining sale price
Final value fee (fixed-price listing: all other categories)	Based on final selling price.	Items sold for $0.99–$50.00: 11.0% Items sold for $50.01–$1,000.00: 11.0% of initial $50.00, plus 6.0% of remaining sale price Items sold for $1,000.01 or more: 11.0% of initial $50.00, plus 6.0% of next $50.01–$1,000.00, plus 2.0% of remaining sale price
Buy It Now	Fee to use the Buy It Now option in a traditional auction listing (first 50 BIN listings per month are free)	Buy It Now price $0.99–$9.99: $0.05 Buy It Now price $10.00–$24.99: $0.10 Buy It Now price $25.00–$49.99: $0.20 Buy It now price $50.00 and up: $0.25
Reserve price auction	Additional fee for holding a reserve price auction	Reserve price from $0.01–$199.99: $2.00 Reserve price $200.00 and up: 1.0% of reserve price

NOTE A *reserve price* is a price, above the minimum bid price, that some sellers set below which they don't want to sell the item. Bidding has to reach the (typically undisclosed) reserve price for a buyer to win the auction. Reserve pricing isn't commonly used for lower-priced items, such as most handmade crafts.

There are all manner of fine print associated with these fees, and additional fees you can incur if you choose certain listing enhancements, such as subtitles in your listings. It's probably best to evaluate the official fee structure with a fine-tooth comb; you can view online at http://pages.ebay.com/help/sell/fees.html.

By the way, invoicing on your account occurs once a month for all your activity for the prior month. (That is, you're not billed one auction at a time; all your fees are saved up for the monthly billing cycle.) You'll get an invoice by email detailing your charges for the month; assuming you've set up your account for automatic billing, your account will be charged at that time.

SIGNING UP FOR EBAY

You sign up for eBay by going to eBay's home page (www.ebay.com) and clicking the Register button. When the Register with eBay page appears, as shown in Figure 7.5, enter your street address, email address, and phone number as requested, as well as your desired user ID and password. Click the Submit button, and eBay sends you a confirmation email. Click the appropriate button or link in this email to activate your account.

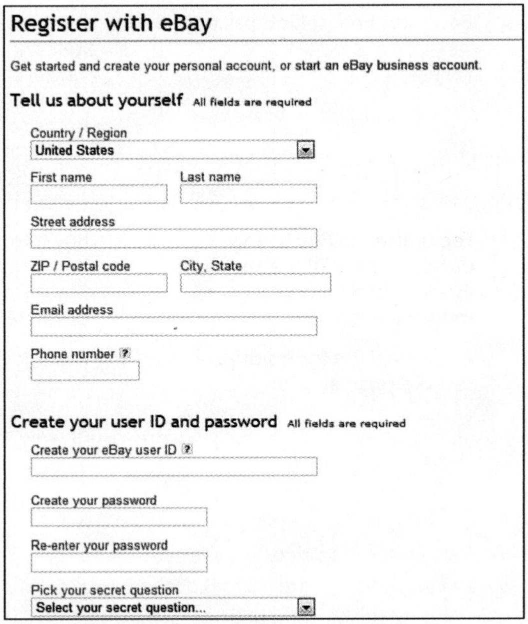

Register with eBay

Get started and create your personal account, or start an eBay business account.

Tell us about yourself All fields are required

Country / Region
United States

First name   Last name

Street address

ZIP / Postal code   City, State

Email address

Phone number ?

Create your user ID and password All fields are required

Create your eBay user ID ?

Create your password

Re-enter your password

Pick your secret question
Select your secret question...

FIGURE 7.5

Registering for eBay.

If you intend to sell items on eBay, you'll need to provide a little bit more information to eBay—in particular, how you want to pay your fees. You do this the first time you list an item for sale.

After you get done creating your very first eBay auction listing, you'll be prompted to create a seller's account. After reviewing your current information on file, eBay will then call you at the phone number you provided and give you a four-digit PIN. Enter this PIN on the next page and click the Continue button.

When the Choose Your Payment Method page appears, select how you wish to pay your eBay fees—PayPal, Credit or Debit Card, or Bank Account. Enter the appropriate information for the payment method you selected, and you're ready to start selling.

LISTING AN ITEM FOR SALE

Once you've signed up and done your homework, listing an item for sale is relatively simple. All you have to do is work through a series of simple forms on the eBay site—although the details differ slightly, depending on which type of listing you want to create.

CREATING AN AUCTION LISTING

To create a basic auction listing, follow these general steps:

1. Click the Sell link in the eBay navigation bar. (If you're not yet logged in to your eBay account, you'll be prompted to do so now.)

2. When the Tell Us What You Sell page appears, enter one or more keywords that describe the item; then click the Search button.

3. eBay now displays one or more categories that might fit the item you're selling, as shown in Figure 7.6. Check the appropriate category or select the Browse Categories tab to browse through other categories. Click the Continue button when done.

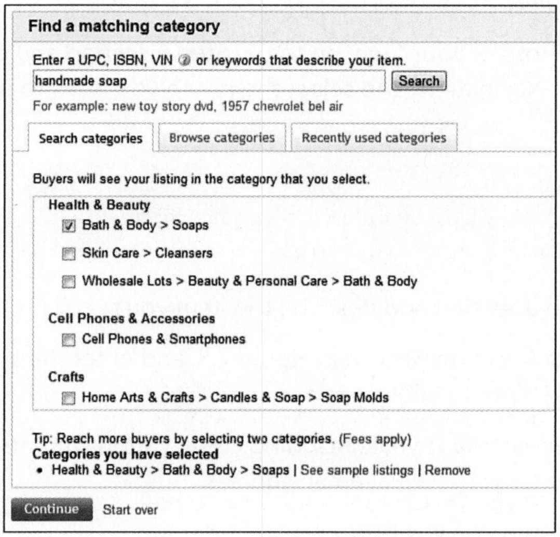

Find a matching category

Enter a UPC, ISBN, VIN ⓘ or keywords that describe your item.

| handmade soap | | Search |

For example: new toy story dvd, 1957 chevrolet bel air

| Search categories | Browse categories | Recently used categories |

Buyers will see your listing in the category that you select.

Health & Beauty
  ☑ Bath & Body > Soaps
  ☐ Skin Care > Cleansers
  ☐ Wholesale Lots > Beauty & Personal Care > Bath & Body

Cell Phones & Accessories
  ☐ Cell Phones & Smartphones

Crafts
  ☐ Home Arts & Crafts > Candles & Soap > Soap Molds

Tip: Reach more buyers by selecting two categories. (Fees apply)
Categories you have selected
 • Health & Beauty > Bath & Body > Soaps | See sample listings | Remove

| Continue | Start over

FIGURE 7.6

Selecting the desired item category.

4. When the Create Your Listing page appears, as shown in Figure 7.7, go to the Step 1 section and enter a descriptive title for your listing into the text box.

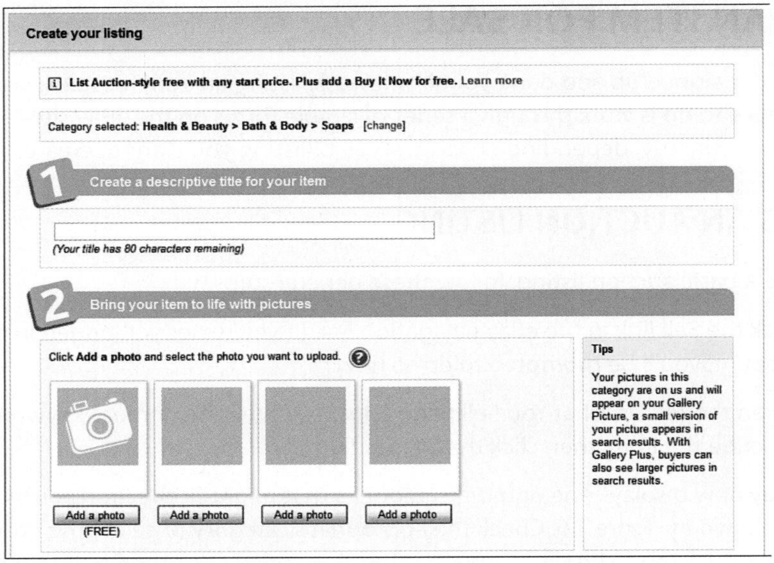

FIGURE 7.7
Creating an item listing.

5. To upload a photo of your item, go to the Step 2 section and click the first Add a Photo button. Navigate to and select the photo you want to upload.

> **NOTE** eBay lets you list up to 12 photos for free.

6. Go to the Step 3 section and describe the item you're selling.

7. Go to the Step 4 section, shown in Figure 7.8, and enter the starting bid, auction duration, and shipping information.

8. To accept payment via PayPal (including credit card payments), go to the Step 5 section and enter your PayPal email address.

9. Click the Save and Preview button.

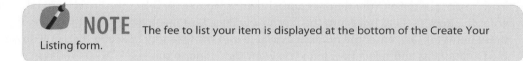

FIGURE 7.8

Determining starting price, auction duration, and shipping.

> **NOTE** The fee to list your item is displayed at the bottom of the Create Your Listing form.

10. When the Review Your Listing page appears, review all listing details and view the preview of how your listing will look. If you need to make changes, click the Edit Listing link. If you like what you see, click the List Your Item button.

eBay creates your item listing and displays a congratulation page. Click the listing title on this page to view the full item listing.

ADDING THE BUY IT NOW OPTION

As noted previously, eBay's Buy It Now option lets you add a fixed-price option to traditional auction listings. The way BIN works is that you name a fixed price for your item; if a user bids that price, the auction is automatically closed and that user is named the high bidder.

> **NOTE** A BIN price is active only until the first bid is placed on an item. If the first bidder places a bid lower than the BIN price, the BIN price is removed and the auction proceeds normally.

You activate the BIN option when you're creating your item listing. Start your listing as described previously, but when you get to Section 4, check the Add Buy It Now to the Listing option and enter the desired Buy It Now price. You can then complete the rest of your listing as normal.

CREATING A FIXED-PRICE LISTING

As you know, eBay also offers the option of creating straight fixed-price listings, with no bidding necessary. These listings look and feel pretty much like standard auction listings, and run for the same length as a standard auction, but feature only the Buy It Now purchase option. Potential buyers can't place bids on these items; they can only purchase the item at a fixed price by clicking the Buy It Now button.

To create a fixed-price listing, you have to use eBay's *advanced* Create a Listing form. You get to this form by clicking the Switch to Form with More Choices at the top of the default Create Your Listing page.

This new form has a lot more options, but the ones we're interested in are in the Choose How You'd Like to Sell Your Item section, shown in Figure 7.9. Select the Fixed Price tab and enter the item's selling price into the Buy it Now Price box. If you have more than one of these items for sale, enter the number available into the Quantity box, and then pull down the Duration list and select how long you want the listing to run—3, 5, 7, 10, 30 days, or Good 'Til Cancelled. Finish the listing as normal, and you're ready to go.

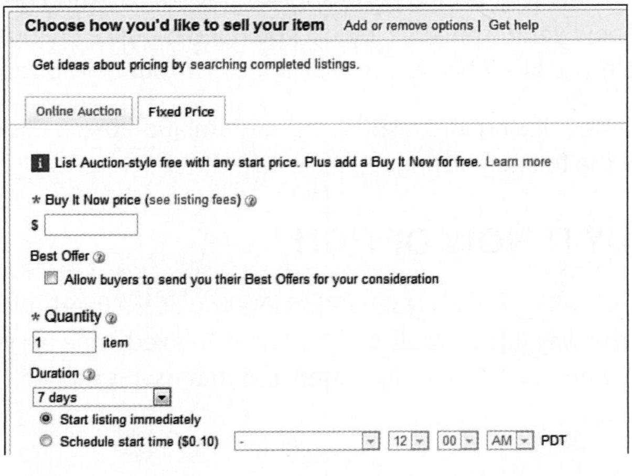

FIGURE 7.9
Entering the selling price for a fixed-price listing.

OPENING AN EBAY STORE

If you list more than 50 items a month, you probably should consider opening your own eBay Store. Anything less, and you're better off with regular fixed-price listings. But once you hit that 50-listing mark, you can actually cut your costs—and offer a more compelling shopping experience—by going the Store route.

WHAT IS AN EBAY STORE?

An eBay Store, like the one shown in Figure 7.10, is a web page that displays all the items you currently have listed for sale, either at a fixed price or via auction. You can organize the items in your Store by your own defined categories.

FIGURE 7.10
The Candles Galore-n-More eBay Store.

As you can see in Figure 7.11, merchants on the eBay Stores home page (stores.ebay.com) are organized by the same categories as the eBay auction site: Antiques, Art, Books, and so on. Buyers can also search for a specific store or a store selling a certain type of item, or view an alphabetical list of all stores.

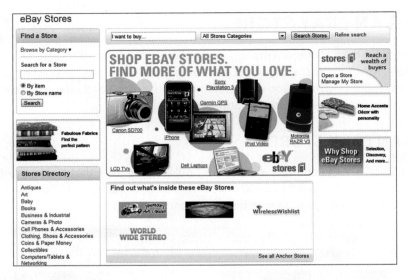

FIGURE 7.11
The home page for eBay Stores.

BENEFITS OF OPENING YOUR OWN EBAY STORE

Why would you want to open your own eBay Store? Well, it certainly isn't for casual sellers; you have to set up your own web page and keep the store filled with merchandise, both of which take time and energy. But if you sell a lot of items each month, there are benefits to opening your own store. They include being able to sell more merchandise (through your store) than you can otherwise sell via single-item listings, being able to offer more merchandise for sale at a lower cost (due to dramatically lower listing fees), and being able to generate repeat business from future sales to current purchasers. In addition, if you do your job right, you can use your eBay Store to sell more merchandise to your existing customers. I think it's the way to go for high-volume crafters.

All this is made feasible—and more profitable—due to the lower costs associated with eBay Store listings. Listing fees for eBay Store items are substantially lower than eBay's normal single-item listing fees—$0.20 per listing vs. the normal $0.50. per listing. This makes the cost of listing on eBay identical to that of Etsy, which is a very good thing; you can afford to list more items for sale without breaking the bank.

In addition, eBay sends all eBay Store owners a monthly Sales Report Plus report. This report provides a variety of data to help you track your Store activity, including total sales; average sales price; buyer counts; and metrics by category, format, and ending day or time. You'll also receive live Traffic Reports that show the number of page views for each of your listings and Store pages, as well as a list of keywords used by buyers to find your listings.

THE COSTS OF RUNNING AN EBAY STORE

Of course, opening an eBay Store costs money. To take advantage of those discounted listing fees, you have to pay a monthly subscription fee. eBay has three subscription levels to choose from—Basic, Featured, and Anchor—as shown in Table 7.2.

Table 7.2   eBay Stores Subscription Levels

	Basic Store	Premium Store	Anchor Store
Subscription fee	$15.95/month	$49.95/month	$299.95/month
Listing fee (fixed-price listings)	$0.20	$0.05	$0.03
Number of product pages per store	Unlimited	Unlimited	Unlimited
Number of custom pages per store	15	15	15
eBay header reduced on Store pages	No	Yes	Yes
Sales management	eBay Selling Manager	eBay Selling Manager Pro	eBay Selling Manager Pro
Markdown Manager for discounted listings	250 listings/day	2,500 listings/day	5,000 listings/day
Picture Pack (12 photos per listing, supersize, and zoom)	Yes	Yes	Yes
Email marketing	5,000 emails/month	7,500 emails/month	10,000 emails/month
Printable promotional flyers and business collateral templates	Yes	Yes	Yes
RSS listing feeds	Yes	Yes	Yes
Rotating placement on eBay Stores home page	No	Text link at center of page	Store logo at top of page
Traffic reports	Basic data	Advanced data	Advanced data

Even when you have an eBay store, you still have to pay eBay for each item you list and each item you sell, as you would with any other type of listing. Aside from the reduced-price listing fees, normal final value fees for fixed-price listings apply.

CHOOSING THE RIGHT SUBSCRIPTION LEVEL

Which of the three Store levels is right for you? eBay recommends the Basic level for merchants listing more than 50 items a month, the Premium level for those listing more than 250 items a month, and the Anchor level for those sellers with very high volumes. For most craft sellers, the Basic level is the place to start. If you find your business ramping up, you can easily switch to the Premium level—and take advantage of those three-cent listing fees.

SETTING UP YOUR STORE

Opening your own eBay store is as easy as clicking through eBay's setup pages. There's nothing overly complex involved; you'll need to create your store, customize your pages (otherwise known as your virtual storefront), and list the items you want to sell. Just follow the onscreen instructions, and you'll have your own store up and running in just a few minutes.

To open your store, start at the eBay Stores main page (stores.ebay.com), and click the Open a Store link. When the next page appears, click Subscribe Now.

On the next page, you choose the subscription level you want—Basic, Premium, or Anchor—and your desired Store name. Next, you choose any additional free products you want (Selling Manager and Sales Reports Plus are offered for free; you might as well take them).

> **NOTE** Selling Manager is a tool that makes it easier to create and manage your listings. Sales Reports Plus is a more sophisticated set of sales reports for your Store.

Next, you accept the user agreement and begin the subscription. At this point, you start building your Store, by entering a Store description, uploading a Store logo, and so on. It's really as simple as filling in the blanks!

LISTING MERCHANDISE FOR SALE

Now that you've created your eBay store, you need to add some merchandise. You do this by clicking the Sell link at the top of any eBay page and creating new fixed-price listings. These listings automatically get placed in your Store.

CUSTOMIZING AND MANAGING YOUR STORE

eBay lets you customize, to some degree, the pages in your eBay Store. You do this by clicking the Seller Manage Store link at the bottom of your Store's home page. This takes you to the Manage Your Store page, where you can customize individual pages in your Store, manage your Store subscription, put your Store on "hold" while you go on vacation, add promotional boxes to pages in your Store, send promotional emails to your customers, and access your eBay Store reports. Just click the appropriate link for the action you want to perform.

GETTING PAID

Unlike Etsy, which lets you accept checks and money orders as payment, eBay only lets buyers pay via credit card (if the seller is set up to accept credit card payments via a merchant account) or PayPal. Naturally, a buyer can use PayPal to make a credit card payment; the buyer pays PayPal via credit card, and PayPal pays the seller via electronic deposit.

> **NOTE** PayPal is actually owned by eBay, and is the default payment processing system on the site.

That's okay, because most online customers pay via credit card, anyway. It's easy enough for a buyer to give PayPal her credit card numbers at the conclusion of a transaction—or, if she already has a PayPal account, to just sign in and let PayPal handle everything.

PayPal charges you, the seller, $0.30 per transaction plus 2.9% of the total transaction price—the item's selling price plus taxes and shipping/handling fees. For example, if you sell an item for $20 with $5 shipping handling, you pay $0.30 plus $0.73 (2.9% of $25), or $1.03 in payment processing fees. These fees are automatically subtracted from the amount that PayPal owes you when an item is paid for.

As a seller, funds from PayPal transactions are placed into your PayPal account almost immediately. You have to manually withdraw those funds, which are then electronically deposited into your chosen bank account. It typically takes 3–5 working days for funds to become available to your bank.

MANAGING YOUR EBAY ACTIVITY

When an item you've listed on eBay is sold (either via Buy It Now or at the end of a successful auction), eBay sends you, the seller, an email to that affect. Most buyers pay immediately at the end of an auction; naturally, anyone purchasing via BIN pays at the time of purchase, as well. As soon as you're notified of payment, you're free to ship the item to the buyer. You're also encouraged to leave positive feedback about that the buyer.

You can monitor the progress of all your current eBay activity via My eBay, a kind of listing management console. Click the My eBay link at the top of any eBay page to display the console; you can then click different tabs to view a Summary of your current activity, all your purchasing activity, all your selling activity, and such.

TIPS FOR MAXIMIZING YOUR EBAY SALES

How do you get the most out of the eBay marketplace? It's similar to selling on Etsy, but with its own unique challenges. Here are a few tips.

PICK THE RIGHT CATEGORY

A quick word about choosing product categories for the items you're selling. Unlike Etsy, which includes common categories for arts and crafts, eBay doesn't. You may have to do a little shoehorning to find the best category for your crafts.

One thing you *don't* want to do is select eBay's Crafts category. This one may seem like the obvious fit, but it isn't. On eBay, the Crafts category is pretty much for craft *supplies*, not for finished crafts. So that one's out.

Instead, pick the existing product category or subcategory that best fits the type of craft you're selling. eBay will suggest categories based on the initial title you enter when creating your listing; if you include the word "handmade" in that title, those suggestions will be more on target.

TIP You can also search eBay before you create your listing for similar crafts. Determine which categories other crafters are using, and use them.

ENHANCE YOUR LISTING DESCRIPTIONS

Unlike some other sites, eBay lets you create fancy item descriptions in a variety of ways. You can enter a simple plain text description, but if you go a little fancier, you can improve your listing's full readership—and, perhaps, improve sales.

First off, you can use formatting controls on the Create Your Listing form, shown in Figure 7.12. The formatting toolbar lets you change font, font size, font color, add bold, italic, or underlined text, and change text alignment. A few clicks of the mouse can make a big improvement in the looks of your item description.

Second, if you're using the advanced listing form and you know a little HTML, you use HTML code to enhance your listing. Just click the HTML tab, shown in Figure 7.13, and insert the appropriate codes for the desired text formatting.

You can also employ the pre-designed themes available with eBay's Listing Designer. As you can see in Figure 7.14, you can choose from a dozen or so fancy formats, for an additional $0.10 a listing.

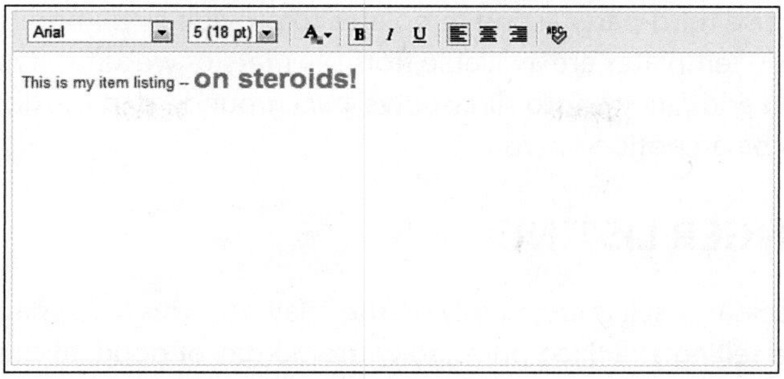

FIGURE 7.12
Use the formatting toolbar to add spice to your item description.

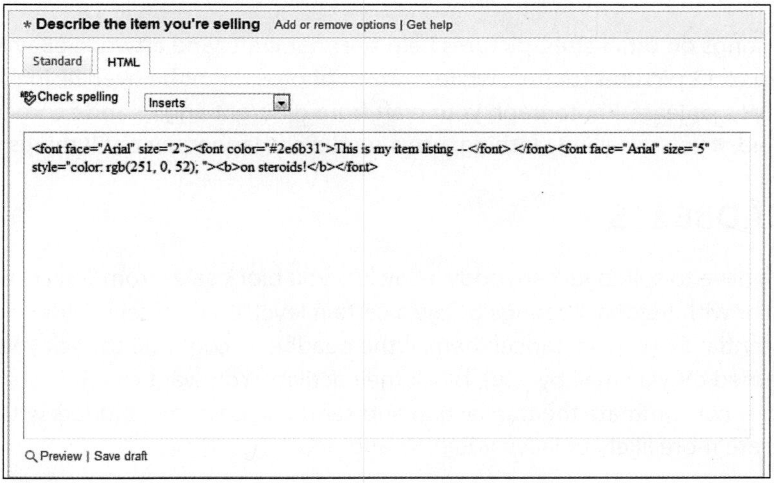

FIGURE 7.13
If you're technically inclined, use HTML to enhance your item description.

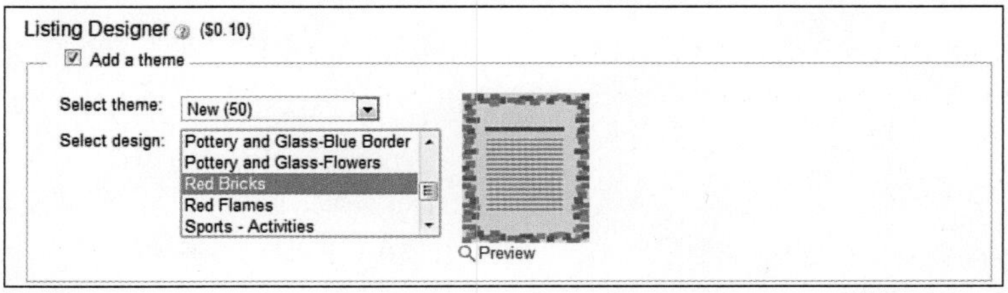

FIGURE 7.14
Listing Designer lets you employ pre-designed templates for your item description.

Finally, you can use third-party listing templates to provide even more sophisticated formatting. These templates are available from a variety of websites, typically for a price, but often let you add fancy photo slideshows, backgrounds, and the like. If you do a lot of listing, this may be an option for you.

CHOOSE A LONGER LISTING

Crafts don't necessarily sell immediately on the eBay site. This argues against shorter item listings. If you're selling at a fixed price, go with a 30-day or good 'til cancelled listing, to give your items enough time to sell.

DON'T FORGET THE PICTURES

As with listings on other sites, pictures help sell your crafts and artwork. eBay lets you upload up to 12 pictures for free; while a dozen photos might be overkill, include two or three photos, at least. Photograph your craft from different angles and zoom into fine details. And, if you're selling clothing, use a model or mannequin to fill things out.

AVOID DEADBEATS

You don't have to sell to just anybody. eBay lets you block sales from buyers with negative feedback or with feedback ratings below a certain level. If you receive bids or orders from these potential deadbeats, cancel them. If the deadbeats continue to click your listings (after being warned off via email by you), block their activity. You want to sell to someone who will actually consummate the transaction and send you payment; bidders with negative feedback are more likely to leave you high and dry.

Selling On Your Own Website

8

If you're fortunate and lots of people start buying your crafts online, you may decide you're better off opening your own ecommerce website. It certainly sounds appealing; you're your own boss, with no fees to pay to any third-party marketplace.

The grass, however, is not always greener. Creating and maintaining your own website takes a lot of time and, yes, money. While you may be able to generate more profit per sale (by not paying any marketplace fees), you also have expenses that you didn't have on Etsy or eBay—as well as the necessity for promoting your site to attract potential customers.

The big question, then, is whether establishing your own website is right for *your* crafts business. Read on and then make up your mind.

BUILDING AN ONLINE STORE—WHAT'S INVOLVED?

Selling on Etsy or eBay is one thing. Selling on your own website is quite another. Just what is involved with building your own ecommerce site—and how much does it cost?

THE COMPONENTS OF AN ECOMMERCE WEBSITE

When you sell on Etsy, eBay, or a similar online marketplace, you're taking advantage of everything these sites offer—the existing infrastructure, the built-in customer traffic, the fully functioning checkout and payment services, you name it. When you launch your own ecommerce website, you have to build all of this from scratch. It won't be easy, but the end result will be *your* online store, one that looks and functions just the way you want it.

What constitutes an online store? To successfully sell merchandise to customers online, every web storefront needs the following components:

- **Site hosting.** First things first—your website needs a home. That means contracting with a website hosting service, to provide storage space and bandwidth. Note that some website hosting services provide services specific to online retailers, offering various selling-related features, such as checkout and payment services—for a price, of course.

- **Domain name registration.** Your website also needs a name. You'll want to register a unique domain name for your site, one that reflects the name and nature of your business. You'll then want to provide that domain name to your site hosting service, so that your site and your name are connected.

> **TIP** Most website hosting services also provide domain name registration, so you can do all this front-end work in a single stop.

- **Home/gateway page.** Every website needs a homepage, but the homepage for a retailer's site is even more important. Your homepage must not only promote your business, but also profile your key products. The page can't be static, either; you need to refresh the featured items on a fairly constant basis, so that returning customers always see something new when they visit. It's easiest if you use some sort of template for the homepage design, into which you can easily place the products you're currently promoting. This argues for some sort of homepage automation, as opposed to you manually recoding the page each time you change featured products.

■ **Navigation and search.** While you may sell some of the products you feature on your site's homepage, it's more likely that customers are going to either browse or search for the specific craft items that they're looking for. That means you need to organize your site in a logical fashion (by craft categories, most likely) and then establish an easy-to-use navigation system that can be accessed from all pages. You'll probably do this via a sidebar or drop-down menu. You'll also need to integrate a search function across your entire site, with a search box at the top of every page that visitors can use to search for specific items.

■ **Product pages.** Every craft you offer for sale should have its own page on your site. That page should be kind of like an Etsy product listing, and with similar information. You need to include one or more product photos, a detailed description, all relevant dimensions and sizes and colors and such, as well as any other information that a customer might need to place an informed order.

■ **Customer reviews.** Many sites let their customers rate and review the products they sell. This provides another key information point for shoppers, as well as offers unique feedback to the seller. While this isn't a necessity, many customers are coming to expect this feature.

■ **Inventory/listing management.** You don't want to manually update your site's product pages whenever you sell an item. Instead, you'll need some sort of automatic inventory and listing management system, where a product sale automatically updates both your inventory database and the "in stock" quantities on your product pages.

■ **Shopping cart and checkout system.** When a customer purchases a product, that product needs to go into that customer's shopping cart—the online equivalent of a physical shopping cart. The cart holds multiple purchases and then feeds into your site's checkout system, which then interfaces with your online payment service.

■ **Payment processing.** If you sell something, you need to get paid. That means, for all practical purposes, accepting credit card payments. While you can try to establish a merchant credit card processing account, more likely you'll sign up with one of the major online payment processing services—PayPal, Google Checkout, or Checkout by Amazon. The payment service you choose should integrate with your own checkout system, so that customers have a seamless purchasing experience.

■ **Customer management.** Your customers will want to contact you with questions or issues. You'll want to contact your customers with purchase confirmation and shipping information. It's best if you can automate all of these customer communications.

In addition to all these necessary components, you'll also need to promote your website; unlike with Etsy and eBay, you won't automatically have millions of qualified customers stopping by your first month in business. That means an investment—in both time and money—in various promotional activities, from pay-per-click advertising to email marketing to whatever works for you.

Bottom line, there's a lot of work required to get an online store up and running—and even more work to keep it running on a daily basis. You're probably used to Etsy or eBay providing most of these pieces and parts and doing most of the heavy lifting for you. When you launch your own web store, however, you're on your own; you have to do everything Etsy and eBay do, and then some.

DIFFERENT WAYS TO BUILD A STORE

How do you go about building your own online store? There are a few different approaches.

First, you can literally build your site from scratch. You start with a blank page and go from there, designing your homepage and product pages, plugging in navigation and search modules, integrating a shopping cart and checkout, and signing up for an online payment service. If you're an HTML master with a lot of time on your hands, you can do this yourself; if you're just a crafter with few if any inherent technical skills, you'll probably hire a website design firm to do most of the work for you. In any instance, going the do-it-yourself route can be quite costly and time consuming—primarily because you're reinventing a lot of wheels as you go along.

For many crafters, a better approach is to go with a prepackaged storefront. When you contract with one of these services, you essentially plug your logo and product inventory into a predesigned store template. Everything you need is provided—automatically generated product pages, inventory and customer management, shopping cart and checkout system, and online payment service. With this kind of service, you can get your site up and running quite quickly, with a minimum amount of effort. The downside of this approach is that you pay for it—and keep on paying for it. Most of these services not only charge you an upfront cost (typically quite low) but also an ongoing commission on everything you sell. In other words, you pay for the convenience of this type of prepackaged storefront.

NOTE Most prepackaged storefronts also lack the full customization you get from creating a completely custom website from scratch.

Between these two extremes is a sort of middle ground. Many third-party services exist that provide the needed features for a quality online storefront, without you having to do the coding from scratch—and without you ceding a portion of your ongoing profits. You simply pick and choose the modules and services you need and plug them into your site. You can find inventory management modules, shopping cart and checkout modules, and the like. (And, of course, it's relatively easy to connect any checkout module with an online payment service.) Depending on the provider(s) you use, you may pay a larger upfront cost with no ongoing fees, or "rent" the services via a monthly or yearly subscription.

HOW MUCH DOES IT COST?

How much you have to invest in an online store depends on the size and nature of the store, as well as the approach you take to constructing the site. That said, I can provide some general cost guidelines.

If you build your site yourself, you don't have any upfront costs save for your domain registration, which can be as little as $10 or so for the first year. You do have, of course, monthly site hosting fees; while some free site hosting services exist, you'll probably spend anywhere from $10 to $50 a month for professional hosting.

More likely, you'll contract out the site design, which costs real money. Depending on the size of the job and the firm you choose, expect to spend several thousand dollars at a minimum. Most design firms charge by the hour, so you'll want to work through an estimate beforehand. Here is where it pays to shop your needs to several design firms and go with the one that not only offers the best price but also is best attuned to your needs.

> **CAUTION** Because of the extremely high design and maintenance costs, most crafters decide against the "from scratch" method of creating an ecommerce website.

The prepackaged storefront route offers perhaps the lowest initial investment—often with *zero* upfront costs. For example, an Amazon Webstore can be had for no money upfront. Instead, you pay $24.99 per month, plus a 2% fee on all sales you make. That's a low-cost way to get into the market, although you have to share your future profits with the storefront host.

If you decide to forgo the prepackaged storefront and instead purchase or subscribe to seller services from third-party providers, your costs are dependent on the services you need, the size of your business, and the provider itself. Some online shopping modules go for as little as $50/month, while larger retailers may end up spending $1,000/month or more.

We then have, of course, those services that charge a fee per transaction. Most notable are the online payment services you need to process credit card transactions. Whether you go with PayPal or one of its competitors, expect to pay anywhere from 2% to 3% of each transaction if paid for via credit card, perhaps with a 30-cent or so flat fee per transaction as well.

With all this said, let's ask that question again: How much does it cost to create your online storefront? As little as nothing or as much as five figures upfront, plus (perhaps) monthly fees and transaction fees and commissions. So if you think that establishing your own storefront frees you from all those niggling fees that Etsy and eBay charge, think again; nothing is free.

PROS AND CONS OF RUNNING YOUR OWN WEBSITE

As you can see, running your own ecommerce website—your own online store—is certainly doable, even if it takes a bit of work. But *should* you do it? Do the pros outweigh the cons?

PROS OF RUNNING YOUR OWN ONLINE STORE

There are many benefits to being your own boss, which is essentially what you get when you run your own online craft store. Here are some of the good points:

- **You create your own business identity.** This is a big one. When you sell on Etsy, eBay, and similar marketplaces, you're often viewed as just another Etsy or eBay seller, no matter how hard you try to establish your own identity. But when you create your own website, you're not part of any marketplace—you're not an Etsy seller or an eBay seller, you are your own business. You can establish your brand however you like and finally be able to build your own business on your own name.

- **You pay fewer transaction fees.** Well, at least you might, depending on how you do things. It's tempting to think that running your own website means escaping all the annoying and costly fees charged by Etsy and (especially) eBay, and that's mostly true. While you can't fully escape all fees (you'll still have to pay a fee for credit card transactions), it's likely you can at least reduce the per-transaction fees you pay.

- **You're not beholden to a marketplace's rules.** Many sellers chafe under Etsy's and eBay's various rules and regulations. You can't do this, you have to do that; you're not really in charge of your business, Etsy or eBay is. Well, when you're running your own website, you're not beholden to anyone but yourself. You make up the rules, you run your business as you please. You're finally free!

In general, then, moving from Etsy or eBay to your own online store means freedom— freedom from rules and regulations, freedom from control, freedom from fees. There is a price to pay for this freedom, however—which is one of the cons we discuss next.

CONS OF RUNNING YOUR OWN ONLINE STORE

If running your own online craft store was so great, everybody would be doing it—and everybody isn't. All the benefits of running your own ecommerce website are counterbalanced by a few negatives. These include the following:

- **It's a lot of effort—both upfront and on an ongoing basis.** When you run your own online store, you have to do everything that Etsy and eBay do—and that's a lot. In fact, you don't really start to appreciate those sites until you have to do it all yourself. You may find that it's worth paying a few Etsy or eBay fees to receive all the benefits you get from those marketplaces. In any case, get ready to start putting in longer hours when you're running your own shop; a lot of time and effort is required.

- **There may be substantial upfront costs.** Depending on the route you go, you may have to invest a substantial amount of money upfront to get your site up and running. If you go completely from scratch (that is, eschew the prepackaged storefront approach), you could spend $10,000 or more to create a unique and fully functioning website. That's not small change, folks.

- **There may be ongoing fees.** Let's say you don't have all that money to invest upfront. Instead, you go with a prepackaged storefront or contract out for various prepackaged ecommerce services. This lets you get into the game without a big upfront investment, but instead you have to pay ongoing monthly fees to use those services. Sometimes the fees are a flat monthly subscription, sometimes the fees are a commission on what you sell; in any instance, make sure you don't pay more in fees for your own site than you did in the Etsy or eBay marketplaces.

- **You still have to pay for credit card sales.** Here's one you can't get away from. Some of the most disliked fees on Etsy and eBay are payment processing fees; some sellers just don't get that you have to pay for the privilege of accepting credit card orders. To that end, the 2.9% you pay to PayPal or Google Checkout isn't that out of line. It's likely you'll pay at least 2% for third-party credit card processing, probably more. You may also be stuck (or prefer to go) with PayPal on your site—which means you still pay that dreaded 2.9% fee per transaction. Get used to it.

- **You won't have any customers on day one.** One of the primary advantages of selling on Etsy or eBay is that you get to tap into their huge established customer base. Millions of potential customers come to those sites every day, looking to buy something; it's a great place for a seller to be. Unfortunately, when you create your own online store, you don't have those millions of visitors. In fact, you don't have *any* visitors on day one. How do you get customers to your site? That leads us to our next disadvantage…

- **You have to promote your own business.** Smart sellers know that the perceived exorbitant fees they pay to Etsy and eBay are primarily not service fees, but rather advertising. That is, they pay to have Etsy or eBay drive business to their product listings. Well, on your own website, you have to do all the promotion yourself. That means paying for pay-per-click or display ads, organizing your own email mailing lists, doing all your own online public relations, you name it. If you have a marketing degree, this is probably second nature to you; if not, you may be in over your head. And whether you know what you're doing or not, it costs time and money to conduct a full-fledged online marketing campaign. How much money do you have in your marketing and advertising budget?

■ **You're not completely your own boss.** So you got yourself out from under the yoke of Etsy or eBay to be your own boss. Good for you! Except that you're never totally your own boss. You're still at the mercy of your customers, of course; if you can't make them happy, they'll find a way to get back at you. (And you won't get any new ones, either.) Plus there are various restrictions you may have to follow if you subscribe to a storefront service; there may even be rules that your web hosting service enforces. And, of course, your online payment service will tell you various things that you can and can't do when accepting payments. It's not quite like being a slave to Etsy or eBay, but it's not that different, either. Meet the new boss, same as the old boss.

Put simply, running your own online craft store will take a lot more time and effort and money than you probably expect—and you may not have the specific expertise required. Are you really ready to run everything yourself? Some crafters are, some crafters aren't. That's a judgment you need to make.

DOES AN ONLINE STORE MAKE SENSE FOR YOUR CRAFTS?

Pros and cons weighed, it's time for the tough question. Does it make sense for you to abandon Etsy and eBay and build your own online craft store? As with all questions of this nature, it depends.

To my mind, the key consideration is your own experience and skill set. Etsy and eBay make selling relatively easy; selling on your own website is a lot harder.

You see, the fees that you pay to Etsy and eBay and other online marketplaces pay for what is really an easy selling environment. You don't have to do a lot more than put together an item listing in order to sell on these marketplaces; practically anyone can do it, to some degree of success.

In fact, Etsy and eBay make selling so easy that it's a relatively level playing field. That makes it fairly easy for the little guys to compete with the big guys, even if they're not particularly skilled or experienced. Just follow the rules and you'll do okay.

The same cannot be said for selling on your own website. If you're not an experienced retailer or trained businessperson, you'll quickly find yourself over your head with your own online store. There's a lot involved; it's running a real business, complete with all the issues and headaches that entails. If you're not prepared for that, you can fail spectacularly.

To run a successful online store, you need to treat it like a real business—because it *is* a real business. That means creating a business plan, arranging proper financing, researching site design and product sales, closely managing the day-to-day operations, devising compelling marketing campaigns and promotional activities, and providing exemplary customer service. You don't have to worry about much or any of these things when you're selling on Etsy or eBay, but it's all there every day when you're running your own site.

And that highlights another issue. For most crafters, the fun part of the endeavor is the crafting itself; selling those crafts is a bit of a chore. Well, selling crafts on your own website is even more of a chore, a really big one, that takes valuable time away from the art of crafting. You may find yourself spending more time running your online store than you do crafting, and that's probably not what you had in mind.

So my advice is simple. If you have formal business training or previous business experience, by all means consider creating your own ecommerce website. But if your business experience consists only of selling via Etsy or eBay, think twice before you go this route. It's a big jump from Etsy and eBay to your own website—and it may not be worth the effort, expense, and risk. Make sure you know what you're getting into before you're in too deep.

CHOOSING A HOSTING SERVICE

Caveats aside, I know a lot of crafters who are big enough and savvy enough that selling via their own online stores makes sense. Assuming that you don't go the "from scratch" route, you want to choose a company to help you build and host your ecommerce website.

The good news is, there are lots of these website hosting companies out there. Most of these companies offer similar features—the hosting itself, of course, as well as catalog/product listing pages, shopping cart and checkout services, even connections to online payment services. Some firms go above and beyond the call of duty by also providing their own online marketplace for the sites they host, as well as additional marketing and promotional services.

You can pay anywhere from $5 to $150 per month for ecommerce hosting; some sites also charge a commission on each transaction you make. In some instances, the monthly fee varies depending on how many items you have for sale. In other instances, the monthly fee varies depending on what ecommerce services you use. It's a big smorgasbord.

FEATURES TO LOOK FOR

As you might suspect, the online store you build is going to be different from the one another seller might build. You may need some services but not others; some features offered may be totally unimportant to you, while others may be essential.

Let's look, then, at what you're likely to find when you go shopping for ecommerce hosting services. Here are some of the more popular features:

- **Site design tools.** Of course, any full-service ecommerce hosting firm is going to offer various tools to help you design your online store. If the site is simple and template driven, this might take the shape of a series of online forms that let you pick and choose from various design options. Other providers might offer software or web-based HTML editing tools for more customized sites. Make sure the hosting firm provides the tools you need to create the type of site you want.

- **Product listing/creation.** If you're selling items online, you have to create selling pages for those items. Find out exactly how a hosting provider lists the items you have for sale—what the product pages look like and what you have to do to create those pages. This is especially important if you have a lot of different craft items for sale; the ability to create quickly hundreds of product pages is more important to you than to another business that only has a few dozen items for sale. In fact, you may want to be able to generate product pages on the fly as you upload your inventory lists, thus creating dynamically generated web pages for your customers.

TIP While you're at it, see how many items the hosting service lets you list. Some lower-priced plans only let you list a few dozen or at most a hundred items; if you have more items for sale, look for a plan that offers unlimited inventory listings.

- **Inventory management.** If you have a large number of items for sale, you want to be able to manage that inventory quickly and easily. Find out how you upload new inventory listings, how the inventory gets adjusted when a sale is made, and how difficult it is to change pricing or other parameters on an item after it's been listed. The best hosting plans provide robust inventory management modules; the least among them require you to do all the inventory management and simply create product pages from the information you provide.

- **Shopping cart and checkout system.** Every ecommerce hosting service provides a shopping cart and checkout system; you can't run an online store without them. Make sure you try out the system before you sign up, though; you want to make sure that it's a painless process for your customers and that it's easy for them to add more items to their orders as they should.

> ✂ **TIP**   Make sure that the checkout system includes secure ordering for your customers.

■ **Payment processing.** Getting paid is a good thing. With an online store, that means accepting credit card payments. Many ecommerce hosting services tie their checkout systems into PayPal, Google Checkout, or similar payment processing services. Other providers offer their own merchant credit card payment services. Some providers offer various alternatives and let you choose the one that best fits your business needs. Make sure you like the options offered—and factor the per-transaction and possible monthly fees into your expense plan.

> 🖌 **NOTE**   Don't assume that a merchant account costs less on a per-transaction basis than PayPal; it isn't necessarily so. Learn more in Chapter 9, "Handling Online Payments."

■ **Order processing and management.** After a customer purchases an item from your site, what happens next? Ideally, you get notified of the sale and how and when it should be shipped. You may even get some shipping assistance, in the form of printing shipping labels with pre-paid postage. Check to see just what sort of order processing the ecommerce hosting firm offers.

■ **Automated customer service.** How do you interact with your customers? Many ecommerce hosting firms offer pre-designed forms that your customers can use to contact you or leave feedback. You may also want to investigate features such as customer message boards, customer product reviews, and the like that you can integrate into your site.

■ **Online marketplace placement.** Some ecommerce hosting firms simply set you up with a website at the domain of your choice. Others link together all their clients into their own online directories or marketplaces. (And, as we'll soon see, some have a particular craft focus.) See what's available; it may be worth paying a little more to a provider that gives you increased visibility in this fashion.

■ **Marketing services.** With some ecommerce hosting firms, you're on your own in terms of promoting your site. Other providers, however, offer a variety of promotional services, including email marketing, search engine optimization, submittal to online shopping sites, and so forth. Check to see what's available—and what you need.

■ **Reporting.** The final thing to look at is one of the most important. You need robust reporting capabilities to track the success of your business—and to help you manage sales and inventory. Take a good look at the reports and analyses offered, and make sure they're all that you need. (It helps if the reports can be customized— and downloaded to your computer in Excel format for your own further analysis.)

> **TIP** If you use QuickBooks for your business' accounting, make sure the site offers QuickBooks integration so you can easily port your data into your accounting software.

In addition to picking and choosing the features you need, you also need to evaluate how easy a firm is to work with. That includes not only the ease of creating a website, but also the technical support and customer service offered to you. If you run into any problems along the way (not just building the site, but also after you're up and running—like if your site goes down in the middle of the holiday shopping season), you want to be able to talk to a live human being and get the problem resolved lickety-split.

COMPARING PRICES

Even though most providers offer similar services, comparing prices between them is a little like comparing apples and penguins; it's often difficult to do a head-to-head pricing comparison because of the ways they approach their fees. For example, some firms charge a setup fee, while some don't; some have a lower monthly subscription fee but a higher sales commission, while others have a higher monthly subscription fee but no sales commission; and there's even one company (Amazon) that doesn't charge any payment processing fees— but makes up for it with much higher transaction fees. It's all a bit confusing.

That said, Table 8.1 provides as close a comparison as possible between the major ecommerce hosting services. Note that pricing can and probably will change over time, and that this table doesn't represent every single firm out there offering these services; it's just a snapshot in time.

Table 8.1   Ecommerce Hosting Price Comparison

Hosting Service	URL	Maximum Number of Products	Setup Fee	Monthly Subscription Fee	Sales Commission/ Transaction Fee	Payment Processing Fee
Amazon Webstore	webstore.amazon.com	Unlimited	$0	$24.95	2.0%	2.9% + $0.30
Big Cartel Gold	www.bigcartel.com	5	$0	Free	0	2.9% + $0.30 (PayPal)

Hosting Service	URL	Maximum Number of Products	Setup Fee	Monthly Subscription Fee	Sales Commission/ Transaction Fee	Payment Processing Fee
Big Cartel Platinum	www.bigcartel.com	25	$0	$9.99	0	2.9% + $0.30 (PayPal)
Big Cartel Diamond	www.bigcartel.com	100	$0	$19.99	0	2.9% + $0.30 (PayPal)
BizHosting Value Hosting Package	www.bizhosting.com	250	$0	$24.95	0	3.5% + $0.35 + $2.49/month (ProPay)
BizHosting Professional Hosting Package	www.bizhosting.com	1,000	$0	$49.95	0	3.5% + $0.35 + $2.49/month (ProPay)
CoreCommerce Pioneer	www.corecommerce.com	150	$0	$19.99	0	2.9% + $0.30 (PayPal or Google Checkout)
CoreCommerce Advanced	www.corecommerce.com	500	$0	$34.99	0	2.9% + $0.30 (PayPal or Google Checkout)
CoreCommerce Professional	www.corecommerce.com	1,500	$0	$59.99	0	2.9% + $0.30 (PayPal or Google Checkout)
Create a Booth	www.createabooth.com	Unlimited	$0	$5.00	0	2.9% + $0.30 (PayPal)
eBay ProStores Starter	www.prostores.com	20	$0	$9.95	1.5%	2.9% + $0.30 (PayPal)
eBay ProStores Business	www.prostores.com	10,000	$0	$29.95	0.5%	2.9% + $0.30 (PayPal)
eCRATER	www.ecrater.com	Unlimited	$0	Free	0	2.9% + $0.30 (PayPal or Google Checkout)
Homestead SimpleStore	www.homestead.com	100	$0	$9.99	0	2.93% + $0.30 + $12.95/month (QuickBooks Merchant Services)
Homestead StoreFront Professional	www.homestead.com	Unlimited	$0	$29.99	0	2.93% + $0.30 + $12.95/month (QuickBooks Merchant Services)
InstantEcom	www.instantecom.net	500	$0	$29.95	0	2.9% + $0.30 (PayPal)
Miva Merchant Boutique	www.mivamerchant	Unlimited	$0	$49.95	0	Variable, via Chase Paymentech (PayPal, Google Checkout, and Checkout by Amazon also available)
Network Solutions Starter	www.networksolutions.com/e-commerce/	25	$49	$29.95	0	2.9% + $0.30 (PayPal or Google Checkout)
Network Solutions Standard	www.networksolutions.com/e-commerce/	300	$49	$56.19	0	2.9% + $0.30 (PayPal or Google Checkout)

Table 8.1   Ecommerce Hosting Price Comparison   continued

Hosting Service	URL	Maximum Number of Products	Setup Fee	Monthly Subscription Fee	Sales Commission/ Transaction Fee	Payment Processing Fee
PrestoStore	www.prestostore.com	Unlimited	$0	$29.95	0	2.9% + $0.30 (PayPal or Google Checkout)
Shopify Basic	www.shopify.com	100	$0	$29.00	2.0%	2.9% + $0.30 (PayPal or Google Checkout)
Shopify Professional	www.shopify.com	2,500	$0	$59.00	1.0%	2.9% + $0.30 (PayPal or Google Checkout)
Vendio Stores Bronze	www.vendio.com	200	$0	$99.95	0	2.9% + $0.30 (Google Checkout)
Vendio Stores Silver	www.vendio.com	2,500	$0	$149.95	0	2.9% + $0.30 (Google Checkout)
Volusion Steel	www.volusion.com	100	$0	$19.00	0	2.9% + $0.30 (PayPal or Google Checkout)
Volusion Bronze	www.volusion.com	500	$0	$39.00	0	2.9% + $0.30 (PayPal or Google Checkout)
Volusion Silver	www.volusion.com	1,000	$0	$59.00	0	2.9% + $0.30 (PayPal or Google Checkout)
Yahoo! Merchant Starter	smallbusiness.yahoo.com/ ecommerce/	50,000	$0	$39.95	1.5%	2.9% + $0.30 (PayPal)
Yahoo! Merchant Standard	smallbusiness.yahoo.com/ ecommerce/	50,000	$0	$99.95	1.0%	2.9% + $0.30 (PayPal)

So which of these firms offer the best deal? It depends, on some degree, to the number of individual products you stock and the amount of monthly sales you hope to conduct. In addition, the range of features and services offered by each company do differ to some degree, so you may have to pay extra to get exactly what you want. Finally, some companies (such as Amazon and eBay) offer optional visibility on their main online marketplaces, whereas with most firms, you're pretty much on your own in terms of attracting customers. Again, you pay for this service.

TIP   Several of these services specialize in sites for artisans and crafters. In particular, check out Big Cartel, Create a Booth, and eCRATER, all of which are relatively low cost (or free!) and feature site designs and other functionality that work well with craft sellers.

Handling Online Payments

9

Whether you're selling your crafts on a marketplace such as Etsy or eBay, or on your own website, when you make a sale you expect to get paid. *How* you get paid is up to you. (And, if you're on an online marketplace, dependent on what payment options that marketplace offers, of course.)

In many cases, you can choose to get paid the old-fashioned way, by cash or check, although that's rapidly going out of fashion. Most online shoppers today prefer to pay via credit card, as it's more convenient and safer for them. The challenge, then, is setting things up so that you, a humble crafter, can accept credit payments.

Fortunately, you have options.

EXAMINING YOUR OPTIONS

The payment options available to you differ by where you sell. Options for eBay sellers are slightly different than for Etsy sellers, and even more different than if you sell via your own craft website. So before you examine all the possible payment methods, check with the marketplaces you use and find out what payment methods they accept.

Now, onto the various payment options. First, know that payment by cash or check not only isn't that popular with shoppers, it also isn't available at all online marketplaces. While Etsy lets you get paid via cash or check, eBay doesn't; it requires all payments to be made via credit card. So check with your chosen marketplaces to see what payment options they offer and prefer.

Second, know that different types of payments have their own pros and cons. While there's something to be said about offering as many payment options as possible (to attract as many customers as possible), some payment options aren't as attractive as others.

To that end, Table 9.1 details the pros and cons of the most popular online payment options.

Table 9.1   Pros and Cons of Common Methods of Payment

Payment Method	Pros	Cons
Cash	No waiting (after payment is mailed), no hassles	Unattractive to buyers (not safe), hard to track, not wise to send cash in the mail
C.O.D.	Cash payment (after item is delivered)	High non-completion rate, lots of paperwork, have to wait longer to receive payment
Personal check	Convenient for buyers	Slow, have to wait for check to clear
Money order/ cashier's check	Fast payment, almost like cash	Hassle for buyers
Credit cards	Fast payment, buyers like it	Fees involved, requires setting up some sort of payment processing system (such as PayPal)

For what it's worth, most online retailers today accept credit card payments and nothing else. In the craft world, it's still possible to deal one-on-one with individual customers, and thus old-school payment methods (cash and money orders, in particular) still have some appeal. While you can offer other payment methods if you like, it's an absolute necessity to accept credit card payments, one way or another.

ACCEPTING CASH, CHECKS, AND MONEY ORDERS

Let's take a quick look at those old-school payment methods—you know, the way everybody *used* to do it. You may choose not to accept these types of payments, or your online marketplace may prohibit you from doing so, but for some sellers they're still viable options.

CASH

Accepting cash payment is standard operating procedure when you sell your goods in person at crafts fairs, open houses, and the like. It's not that popular when selling online, however.

As a seller, there's nothing wrong with opening up an envelope and finding a few crisp new bills inside. But sending cash through the mail is not one of the smartest things an online customer can do; cash is too easily ripped off and virtually untraceable. You can ask for cash payment (not that you should, of course), but unless the selling price for an item is extremely low (under $5), don't expect buyers to comply.

One other thing. Cash is hard to keep track of—even for extremely organized sellers. There's no paper trail, and it's tempting to take any cash you receive and just stuff it in your wallet. If you do receive a cash payment, try your best to treat it like a money order or cashier's check, at least in terms of how you track it.

The bottom line: If it's bad for your customers, it's bad for you too. You should probably discourage payment by cash—unless you're selling via Craigslist and can accept the bills in person.

C.O.D.

Here's a dying method of payment. With cash on delivery (C.O.D.), you ship the item to the buyer, with the stipulation that the deliveryman (or woman) collect payment when the item is delivered.

There are problems with this method, however. What happens if the buyer isn't home when the delivery is made? What if the buyer is at home, but doesn't have the cash? What if the buyer refuses to pay—and rejects the shipment? It happens—a lot.

Even worse, C.O.D. service often comes with a high fee from the carrier—and it's a fee that you, the seller, have to pay. The additional fee alone rules out C.O.D. for many sellers.

Then there's the fact that you don't get your money until after the item is delivered. The delay in your getting your cash reduces the appeal considerably.

All things considered, it's easy to see why few sellers offer C.O.D. payment. The problems with this payment method tend to outweigh the benefits, and I can't recommend it.

PERSONAL CHECKS

It used to be that most customers (online and off) paid most retailers via personal check. That's not the case anymore; checks are a rapidly declining method of payment, both online and in the real world.

There were a few reasons why checks used to be so popular. It's relatively convenient to write a check and either hand it to a store clerk or pop it in an envelope. It's certainly faster to write a check than it is to process a money order. And personal checks can be tracked (or even cancelled) if problems arise with the transaction.

To sellers, however, personal checks are problematic. You see, when you deposit a check in your bank, you're not depositing cash. That $100 check doesn't turn into $100 cash until it tracks back through the financial system, from your bank back to the buyer's bank, and the funds are both verified and transferred. That can take some time, typically 10 business days or so.

CAUTION If a check bounces, the depositor (you) will likely be assessed a fee from your bank. (Of course, the writer of the bad check will also have a fee to pay—but that's not your problem.) If the buyer who wrote the check offers to make good on the payment, make sure they reimburse you for your bad check fee, over and above the final auction price.

Fortunately for us sellers, consumers are writing fewer and fewer checks, preferring electronic payment methods, such as credit cards. You can offer payment by check if you want, but chances are you won't lose any sales if you don't.

If you do decide to accept check payments, deposit any check you receive as soon as possible—but do *not* ship the merchandise. Wait until the check clears the bank (two weeks if you want to be safe—longer for checks on non-U.S. banks) before you ship the item. If, after that period of time, the check hasn't bounced, it's okay to proceed with shipment.

TIP If you are on the bad end of a bounced check, all hope is not lost. The first thing to do is get in touch with your bank and ask them to resubmit the check in question. Maybe the buyer was just temporarily out of funds. Maybe the bank made a mistake. Whatever. In at least half the cases, bounced checks unbounce when they're resubmitted.

MONEY ORDERS AND CASHIER'S CHECKS

Money orders and cashier's checks are, to sellers, almost as good as cash. You can cash a money order immediately, without waiting for funds to clear, and have cash in your hand. When you receive a money order or cashier's check, deposit it and then ship the sold item. There's no need to hold the item for the check to clear.

The only bad thing about money orders and cashier's checks is that you have to wait for them to arrive. Even if the buyer puts payment in the mail the very next day, you'll still wait anywhere from 3 to 5 days after the auction to receive payment. Still, there's not a lot to dislike about this method of payment—it's hard to get burned with either a money order or cashier's check.

> **CAUTION** It is possible to receive a bad cashier's check. That's because a cashier's check or money order isn't *exactly* the same as cash; your bank still needs to be reimbursed by the issuing institution, and if this doesn't happen, the cashier's check/money order will bounce—although this is highly unlikely. Be particularly careful of money orders or cashier's checks drawn on foreign banks, or issued by unfamiliar institutions. When in doubt, hold the merchandise and ask your bank to verify that the payment is good.

CREDIT CARDS

Until just a few years ago, if you wanted to accept credit card payment for online sales, you had to be a big-time retailer, complete with merchant account and bank-supplied charge card terminal. Fortunately, that's not the case today; there are several options available that enable you to accept credit card payments for the items you sell. (Figure 9.1 shows the big four credit cards you want to accept—MasterCard, Visa, American Express, and Discover.)

FIGURE 9.1

You want to accept credit card payments from your customers.

The most popular option is to sign up with an online payment processing service, such as PayPal, that accepts credit card payments on your behalf. Your customer provides her credit card number to processing service, the service processes the payment, and then the service deposits the resulting funds into your bank account. You don't have to do much of anything, save pay the processing service's fees; the payment processing service serves as the "middle man" for the transaction, both processing the order (using its own checkout system) and accepting the customer's payment.

You may also have the option of establishing your own merchant credit card account. You may be able to do this with your local bank, or with an independent merchant credit card processing company that acts as a bridge between you and the large credit card companies. Know, however, that banks and independent processors typically deal with larger retailers, not with small craft sellers; this may be a dead end.

However you go, you will pay a fee for accepting credit card payments. Expect to pay around 3% of the total transaction price, plus a small flat per-transaction fee, typically around $0.25 or $0.30. That's how the payment processing companies make their money.

EXAMINING THE BIG PAYMENT PROCESSING SERVICES

There are three big payment processing services today that handle the bulk of online payments for small merchants and individual sellers. PayPal, Google Checkout, and Checkout by Amazon all offer similar services to sellers and their customers; we'll look at each in turn.

PAYPAL

The most-used online payment processing service is PayPal. Even though PayPal is owned by eBay, it processes payments for all manner of online sellers, large and small.

PayPal accepts customers payments via American Express, Discover, MasterCard, and Visa, as well as electronic bank transfers. While PayPal is a U.S.-based service, it also accepts payments to or from close to 200 countries and regions in more than 20 different currencies—which makes it relatively easy to accept payments from customers outside the United States.

NOTE Before you can use PayPal to accept payments, you must sign up for the PayPal service. Some online marketplaces facilitate this process for you; in other cases, you need to go to PayPal's website and sign up manually. Learn more at www.paypal.com.

PayPal, like all online payment services, charges the seller for every transaction made. The buyer doesn't pay any PayPal fees—although he still has to pay finance charges to his own credit card company, of course.

As a merchant, you pay a percentage of the total transaction, plus a flat per-transaction fee. Note that the fees you pay are based on the *total amount of money transferred paid*—that's the selling price plus any taxes and shipping/handling fees. So, for example, if you sell a $10 item and charge $0.50 tax and a $5 shipping/handling fee, the buyer pays PayPal a total of $15.50—and PayPal bases its fee to you on that $15.50 payment.

PayPal's fees range from 2.2% to 2.9%, depending on your monthly sales volume. Table 9.2 presents PayPal's fee schedule as of August 2012.

Table 9.2   PayPal Transaction Fees (U.S.)

Monthly Sales	Transaction Fee
$0–$3,000.00	2.9% + $0.30
$3,000.01–$10,000.00	2.5% + $0.30
$10,000.01+	2.2% + $0.30

> **NOTE** Most craft sellers fall in the lower range and will pay the 2.9% rate. All fees are deducted from your account with every transaction.

Let's do an example transaction. Let's say you sell an item for $10, with a $5 shipping/handling fee. The total that the buyer pays is $15 (there's no sales tax involved); it's this amount on which your fees are based. Assuming that you're in PayPal's first payment tier (under $3,000 a month), you pay 2.9% of that $15, or $0.44, plus the $0.30 transaction fee. Your total fees for that transaction: $0.74.

When a customer pays for an item via PayPal, using a payment button like the one in Figure 9.2, those funds are immediately transferred to your PayPal account, and you receive an email notification of the payment. This email will include all the information you need to ship the item to the buyer.

FIGURE 9.2

Customers check out by clicking the PayPal button.

You have to manually withdraw the funds due to you from PayPal; no automatic payment option is available. You can let your funds build up in your PayPal account, or you can choose (at any time) to withdraw all or part of your funds.

> **TIP** I recommend clearing your PayPal account at the end of each business day. There's no reason to let PayPal hold onto your money any longer than necessary.

You have the option of okaying an electronic withdrawal to your checking account (no charge; takes three to four business days) or requesting a check for the requested amount ($1.50 charge; takes one to two weeks). You handle this and other account maintenance transactions directly from the PayPal website.

> **NOTE** If you have your own ecommerce website, learn more about using PayPal in my companion book, *The PayPal Official Insider Guide to Growing Your Business* (Michael Miller, PayPal Press/Peachpit Press, 2011).

GOOGLE CHECKOUT

While PayPal is the most popular online payment service today, it does have competition. PayPal's chief competitor is Google, in the form of Google Checkout (checkout.google.com/sell/). Google Checkout functions in much the same manner as PayPal, offering checkout and payment services for Internet retailers of all shapes and sizes; like PayPal, Google Checkout lets buyers pay via Visa, MasterCard, American Express, and Discover cards. All they have to do is click the Google Checkout button shown in Figure 9.3.

FIGURE 9.3
Customers check out by clicking the Google Checkout button.

> **NOTE** Google Checkout is part of Google Wallet, Google's online payment service for consumers.

NOTE Unlike PayPal, Google Checkout doesn't offer payment via e-check or electronic bank withdrawal. And, at present, Google Checkout is only available to United States and United Kingdom merchants; it doesn't offer PayPal's international payment options.

For sellers, Google Checkout offers the same type of checkout and payment services offered by PayPal. Pricing is virtually identical to that offered by PayPal, with the addition of slightly deeper discounts for larger merchants, as detailed in Table 9.3.

Table 9.3   Google Checkout Transaction Fees (U.S.)

Monthly Sales	Transaction Fee
$0–$3,000	2.9% + $0.30
$3,000–$9,999.99	2.5% + $0.30
$10,000–$99,999.99	2.2% + $0.30
$100,000+	1.9% + $0.30

To use Google Checkout for website payments, you first need to sign up for the service. The process is similar to what you go through when you first set up a PayPal account. The on-going payment process is also similar to PayPal's.

Knowing how similar these services are, why would you choose Google Checkout over PayPal? Frankly, I'm not sure. When Google Checkout first started out, they offered lower seller fees, but that's not the case today. With near-identical fee structures and services, you can't go wrong with either service—although it's worth noting that PayPal has much more name recognition and acceptance with online shoppers.

CHECKOUT BY AMAZON

There's a new contender in the online payment service wars, and it's a name you know. Checkout by Amazon puts Amazon.com's vaunted checkout process on any ecommerce website, providing customers a familiar experience and you an end-to-end shopping cart/checkout solution, complete with credit card processing. (Figure 9.4 shows a Checkout by Amazon payment button.)

FIGURE 9.4
Customers check out by clicking the Amazon button.

While you probably won't find Checkout by Amazon as an option at your favorite online marketplace, it is a viable option if you host your own online craft store. In general, the fees for using Checkout by Amazon are right in line with those you pay for using PayPal. There are some exceptions to the rule, but if you're selling items that cost $10 or more, you pay 2.9% of the total transaction cost plus 30 cents per transactions. That's identical to PayPal fees.

In addition, Checkout by Amazon is a great shopping cart and checkout process for customers. If you've ever shopped at Amazon yourself, you know what I mean. In fact, if your customers are also Amazon customers, they can check out using their Amazon information. For these joint customers, you also have the option of offering 1-click ordering, just like Amazon does on its site. In addition, Amazon offers your customers its own purchase protection plan, which is a nice bonus.

Let's take a closer look at those transaction fees. Like PayPal, the fees go down the more business you do. Table 9.4 provides the details.

Table 9.4   Checkout by Amazon Fee Structure

Monthly Sales Volume	Percentage of Transaction	Per-Transaction Fee
< $3,000	2.9%	$0.30
$3,000–$10,000	2.5%	$0.30
$10,000–$100,000	2.2%	$0.30
$100,000+	1.9%	$0.30
Any transaction of less than $10	5.0%	$0.05

Amazon charges no set-up fee or monthly subscription fee. You get charged only for those transactions your customers complete. Your funds are then automatically deposited into your checking account, via electronic transfer.

For your part, you're notified by email when an order has been placed. You then pack and ship the item, and wait for Amazon to deposit your funds into your checking account.

Again, given the similar pricing between Checkout by Amazon and PayPal, why choose one over another for your ecommerce website? It's really a matter of which gigantic huge company you best like dealing with—and which checkout system you think your customers might be more comfortable with.

Shipping Your Merchandise

10

For many crafters, the most challenging aspect of the selling experience isn't the selling of an item, it's getting that item packed and shipped to the customer. Let's face it, packing fragile crafts items isn't always easy, and choosing the right shipping service (and calculating shipping fees) can be an exercise in frustration. Most crafters are good at crafting, not at packing and shipping delicate items.

What you need, then, is a little advice on how to pack and ship your craft items in a safe and cost-efficient manner—which I'll provide in this chapter.

CHOOSING A SHIPPING METHOD

You have a number of choices when it comes to shipping the craft items you sell. You can use the various services offered by the U.S. Postal Service (regular mail, Priority Mail, Express Mail, and so on) or any of the services offered by competing carriers, such as UPS or FedEx. You can deal directly with any shipping service or you can use a local shipping store to handle the shipping—and even the packing—for you.

CAUTION Having another company do your packing for you costs money—which is why most crafters prefer to deal directly with their shipping service of choice.

Which service should you use? That's a good question, but not always an easy one to answer. Ultimately, you have to strike a compromise between cost, convenience, and speed. Pick the cheapest method possible, and customers will gripe when they don't receive their merchandise in a timely manner. Pick the fastest method possible, and customers will gripe that they're paying too much for shipping/handling. (You also may turn away potential buyers with your high shipping/handling fees.) Like I said, you need to strike a balance—and also choose a shipper that is easy for you to deal with.

And here's what makes the decision particularly difficult. Once you start checking around, you'll find that shipping rates vary wildly from one service to another—and I mean *wildly*. For example, the costs for shipping a 2 pound box from New York to Los Angeles range from under $6 (USPS Priority Mail in a flat rate envelope) to more than $70 (UPS Next Day Air and FedEx Priority Overnight). That's a *big* difference.

TIP To compare shipping costs for a variety of services on a single web page, check out ShipGooder (www.shipgooder.com). Just enter your ZIP code, the recipient's ZIP code, and the package's weight and size, and ShipGooder creates a table of all available shipping options from the major shipping services.

This variation in shipping costs is a good reason to standardize the type of crafts you sell. If you only offer one or two types of items, you can easily calculate your shipping fees ahead of time. If you're selling a wide variety of items, calculating shipping for all those different items becomes extremely time-consuming. In addition, standardizing the crafts you sell also helps when buying your packing boxes—you only have to buy one or two types of boxes, instead of having to keep a wide variety of packaging on hand.

Of course, cost isn't the only factor you want to consider. You also want to compare how long it takes the package to arrive, what kind of track record the shipping service has, and how convenient it is for you to use. If you have to drive 20 miles to get to a UPS office but you have a post office just down the street, that might offset a slightly higher cost for Priority Mail.

TIP You may need to factor weather conditions into which type of shipping you choose. If it's summertime and you're shipping something that might melt or go bad in extreme heat (like homecooked food items), pick the fastest shipping method possible.

The main thing to keep in mind is that you want to, as much as possible, settle on a single shipper and method of shipping for the items you sell. The last thing you want to do is to make trips to multiple shipping stations each day, and deal with a myriad number of packing boxes and shipping instructions. Standardize on a single shipper and method, and you'll make your shipping "department" much more efficient. Don't, and you'll waste a lot of time unnecessarily.

We'll look at each of the major shipping services separately, but with a decided emphasis on the U.S. Postal Service—which is the shipper of choice for a majority of online craft sellers.

NOTE The cost to ship a particular package is based on a combination of weight, size, and distance; the heavier an item is and the further it has to go (and the faster you need to get it to where it's going), the more it costs. And when you're factoring package size, you'll need to measure the length of the package and add it to the girth. (Length is the longest side of the package; girth is the distance all the way around the package at its widest point perpendicular to the length.)

U.S. POSTAL SERVICE

The United States Postal Service (USPS) is used by many craft sellers for at least some of their shipping needs. Dealing with the Postal Service is convenient, as most sellers have a post office within a short driving distance, and they're set up to easily handle the shipping of small items from individuals.

The Postal Service offers several different shipping options:

- **Priority Mail.** This is the preferred shipping method for a lot of craft sellers, big and small. Pricing is generally quite reasonable, and if you're shipping out a small item that can fit in one of their flat-rate envelopes, you can quote a simple rate of $5.15 (as of summer 2012), anywhere in the nation; use the smallest flat-rate box, shown in Figure 10.1, and ship for just $5.35. Service is typically in the one-to-three day range, and the postal service offers free Priority Mail shipping boxes you can use. You can also print out your own Priority Mail shipping labels and postage, direct from the USPS website, which is uber convenient.

FIGURE 10.1

Ship via USPS Priority Mail and use their free packing boxes.

- **Express Mail.** This is a less-used option, primarily because of its high cost—considerably more expensive than Priority Mail. Express Mail is the Postal Service's fastest service, offering guaranteed next-day delivery 365 days a year, including weekends and holidays. Merchandise is automatically insured up to $100.

- **First Class Mail.** This is an option if your item fits into a standard-sized envelope or small box. It also provides the benefit of shipping directly from your mailbox, without necessitating a trip to the post office—assuming you can figure out the correct postage yourself. Delivery is similar to Priority Mail: typically three days or less. If your item is relatively small, First Class can cost a little less than Priority Mail.

- **Parcel Post.** This used to be known as the "slow" USPS service for larger packages, but it's gotten faster of late—and it's priced much lower than Priority Mail. Still, it might take seven to nine days to ship something Parcel Post from coast to coast, as opposed to Priority Mail's two (or three) days.

You can find out more about USPS shipping at the USPS website, located at www.usps.com. You can also access the USPS Domestic Calculator (postcalc.usps.gov) to calculate postage for all levels of service.

FEDEX

FedEx is probably the fastest shipping service, but it's also the most costly. FedEx tends to target the business market (which can afford its higher rates), so it isn't widely used for retail shipping—with one significant exception.

That said, the FedEx Ground service is much more cost effective when you're shipping out larger items, like the one shown in Figure 10.2. For example, FedEx charges two dollars or so less than Priority Mail to ship a five-pound item from coast to coast. That's a significant saving!

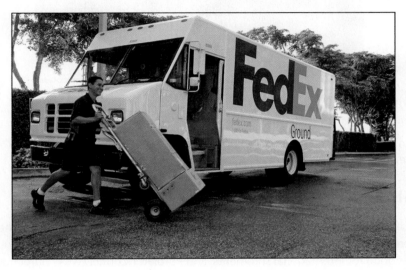

FIGURE 10.2

Check out FedEx Ground when shipping larger and heavier items.

FedEx is also a convenient choice for many sellers, especially since you can ship from any FedEx Office store location. You can find out more about FedEx shipping at its website, located at www.fedex.com, and can access the company's rate finder directly at www.fedex.com/ratefinder/.

UPS

While UPS is a little pricey for small, lightweight items, it's a good option for shipping larger or heavier packages. UPS offers a variety of shipping options, including standard UPS Ground, Next Day Air, Next Day Air Saver, and 2nd Day Air. And you can drop off your items for shipment at any UPS Store, like the one shown in Figure 10.3.

FIGURE 10.3

Ship items from your neighborhood UPS Store.

You can find out more about UPS shipping—and access a rate calculator—at the UPS website, located at www.ups.com.

OTHER SHIPPING COMPANIES

USPS, UPS, and FedEx are the three most popular shipping services in the US; they're not the only services available, however. Among the other services available are DHL (www.dhl.com), which is good for international shipments, and Purolator Courier (www.purolator.com).

> **NOTE** Less-experienced or occasional sellers might choose to do their packing and shipping through a professional shipping store, such as The UPS Store (www.theupsstore.com) or FedEx Office (www.fedex.com/us/office/). Because of the high fees these stores charge, this really isn't a good option for high-volume sellers. Still, you might want to go this route if you have the occasional large or overly fragile item to ship.

CALCULATING SHIPPING AND HANDLING FEES

You need to include all the details about shipping and handling (including and especially shipping costs) up-front in your item listing. While this is a good idea, how do you figure shipping costs before you know where the item is going?

WORKING WITH FLAT FEES

The solution is easy if you're shipping something small and light, like most crafts. Figure the shipping costs from your location to either coast, and either use the highest cost or an average of the two costs. When the shipping is low to begin with, if you're off a dollar one way or another, it's not a big thing.

Flat fees are also easy if you're using one of the postal service's flat-rate Priority Mail packages. They have several different types of boxes and envelopes you can use for their flat-rate shipping. Use one of these containers and anything you can fit inside—no matter what the weight—ships anywhere in the U.S. for that flat rate. It certainly makes it easy to calculate your shipping charges.

DETERMINING THE HANDLING CHARGE

Aside from the pure shipping costs, you should consider adding a handling charge to the shipping fees your customers pay. After all, you need to be sure that you're compensated for any special materials you have to purchase to package the item—labels, boxes, Styrofoam peanuts, and so forth. That doesn't mean you charge one buyer for an entire roll of tape, but maybe you add a few pennies to your shipping charge for these sorts of packaging consumables. And if you have to purchase a special box or envelope to ship an item, you should definitely include that cost in your shipping charge.

So you should have no compunction against "padding" your shipping fees with an additional handling charge—as long as you don't get too greedy. Add 10% or so for handling and no one will complain; double your shipping costs for handling, and you'll be gouging your customers.

> **TIP** If you have multiple items for sale, some customers will purchase more than one item in a single order. If that happens, you don't need to pack two or more separate boxes for that buyer; you can easily pack all the items purchased in a single box, which will reduce shipping costs. You should pass on that savings to that customer, in the form of a combined shipping/handling fee for all items purchased.

PACKING YOUR ITEMS

Packing your merchandise is a lot of work. Let's look at what's involved in packing an item so that it arrives at its destination intact—but doesn't cost you an arm and a leg to get there.

PICKING THE RIGHT SHIPPING CONTAINER

It's important to choose the right type of shipping container for a particular item. It'll save you time and money in the long run.

First, you have to decide whether to use a box or an envelope. If you have a very large item to ship, the choice is easy. But what if you have something smaller and flatter, such as a greeting card or pin? Your choice should be determined by the fragility of your item. If the item can bend or break, choose a box; if not, an envelope is probably a safe choice.

Whichever you choose, pick a container that's large enough to hold your item without the need to force it in or bend it in an inappropriate fashion. Also, make sure that the box has enough extra room to insert cushioning material.

On the other hand, the container shouldn't be so big as to leave room for the item to bounce around. Also, you pay for size and for weight; you don't want to pay to ship anything bigger or heavier than it needs to be.

If you're shipping a breakable or bendable item in an envelope, consider using a bubble-pack envelope (see Figure 10.4) or reinforcing the envelope with pieces of cardboard. This is especially vital if your item shouldn't be bent or folded.

FIGURE 10.4

Ship flat and fragile items in a bubble-pack envelope.

If you're shipping in a box, make sure it's made of heavy, corrugated cardboard and has its flaps intact. Thinner boxes—such as shoe boxes or gift boxes—simply aren't strong enough for shipping. When packing a box, never exceed the maximum gross weight for the box, which is usually printed on the bottom flap.

HOW TO PACK

How do you pack your box?

Don't just drop your item in an empty box; you need to position the item toward the center of the box, away from the bottom, sides, and top, and surround it with cushioning material. Professional shippers use Styrofoam peanuts, like the ones in Figure 10.5, and lots of them; another option is to use crumpled up old newspapers. Know, however, that peanuts are *much* lighter than newspaper. Since weight is a factor in how much you'll pay for shipping, anything you can do to lighten the weight of your package is important. Because peanuts cost… well, *peanuts*, they're the cushioning material of choice.

FIGURE 10.5
Use plenty of padding in your packaging; Styrofoam peanuts will do the job.

If you're shipping several items in the same box, be sure to wrap each one separately (in separate smaller boxes, if you can) and provide enough cushioning to prevent movement and to keep the items from rubbing against each other. Not only should items be separated from each other in the box, but they should also be separated from the corners and sides of the box to prevent damage if the box is bumped or dropped.

The previous point argues for another technique—double boxing especially fragile items such as glass or ceramic items. That means packing the item tightly in a smaller, form-fitting box, and then placing that box inside a slightly larger, shock-absorbing box—with at least 3" of cushioning material between the boxes.

If your item has any protruding parts, cover them with extra padding or cardboard. And be careful with the bubble wrap. Although it's great to wrap around objects with flat sides, it can actually damage more fragile figurines or items with lots of little pieces and parts sticking out. If the bubble wrap is too tight, it can snap off any appendages during rough handling.

When you're packing an item, watch the weight. Have a postal scale at your packing counter, and weigh the item—shipping container and all—during the packing process. With Priority Mail, the difference between shipping a one-pound package and a one-pound, one-ounce package is as much as $4, depending on where it's going. Finding some way to cut that extra ounce of packing material can save almost two bucks in shipping costs!

CAUTION Make sure you include the weight of the box and the packing material when you weigh your item for shipment. A big box with lots of crumpled paper can easily add a half-pound or more to your item's weight—excess weight you'll have to pay for.

After you think you're done packing, gently shake the box. If nothing moves, it's ready to be sealed. If you can hear or feel things rattling around inside, however, it's time to add more cushioning material. (If you can shake it, they can break it!)

ONE SIZE DOESN'T FIT ALL

As you might expect, packing needs vary for different types of items. Here are some tips for packing and shipping specific types of crafts:

- **Cards and other flat paper items.** Shipping in an envelope makes sense, but how do you keep the item from getting bent, folded, and spindled in transit? Cut two pieces of sturdy cardboard about 1/4" larger than the item. Place the item in a plastic Ziplock bag or page protector, and then sandwich it between the two pieces of cardboard. It's also a good idea to tape the cardboard lightly on all four edges to prevent slippage.

- **Clothing.** Standard Priority Mail envelopes and boxes work great for most clothing items. (You can fit many clothing items into the Priority Mail flat-rate envelope!) For single or smaller items, Tyvek envelopes are ideal.

- **Framed artwork.** Take the glass out of the frame and wrap it separately. Do not let artwork come in direct contact with paper or cardboard. Enclose photographs in plastic bag to protect against wetness. You may need to combine two boxes to encase larger paintings and framed items.

- **Glassware and vases.** Stuff hollow items with newspaper, tissue paper, or other packing material; this provides an extra level of cushioning in case of rough handling. Wrap items in tissue paper, bubble wrap, or foam padding, as shown in

Figure 10.6. Use masking tape to affix cut-off paper towel rolls to spouts and handles. Allow at least 3" of cushioning around the item in the box; consider double boxing.

FIGURE 10.6

Wrap glassware in bubble wrap or other protective material.

- ■ **Jars and items with lids.** Either separate the lid from the base with several layers of bubble wrap or tissue paper or (better still) pack the lid in a separate small box.

- ■ **Jewelry.** Use a standard size box that won't draw attention to itself. Do not label the box as to its contents. Insure the package appropriately.

> **TIP**   When you're shipping something that's especially fragile, know that the longer it takes to ship, the more likely it is to get damaged. That argues for choosing a faster shipping service, even if it costs a little more. Speed up the time in transit, and you reduce the odds of it getting bent, folded, spindled, or mutilated by the shipping carrier.

HOW TO SEAL THE PACKAGE

After your box is packed, it's time to seal it. A strong seal is essential, so always use tape that is designed for shipping. Make sure you securely seal the center seams at both the top and the bottom of the box. Cover all other seams with tape, and be sure not to leave any loose tape or open areas that could snag on machinery.

You should use sealing tape designed for shipping, such as pressure-sensitive tape, nylon-reinforced Kraft paper tape, glass-reinforced pressure-sensitive tape, or water-activated paper tape. Whichever tape you use, the wider and heavier, the better. Reinforced is always better than non-reinforced.

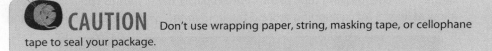

CAUTION Don't use wrapping paper, string, masking tape, or cellophane tape to seal your package.

One last thing: If you plan to insure your package, leave an untaped area on the cardboard where your postal clerk can stamp "Insured." (Ink doesn't adhere well to tape.)

CREATING THE SHIPPING LABEL

You've packed the box. You've sealed the box. Now it's time for the label.

The best-packed box won't go anywhere if you get the label wrong. For fast and efficient delivery, you need to create a label that can be both clearly read and clearly understood. And it goes without saying that the address information needs to be accurate and complete—partial addresses just don't cut it.

To create the perfect label, you need to write, type, or use your computer to print the address as neatly as possible. You should also use complete address information, including all street suffixes—Dr., Ave., St., Blvd., and so on. And make sure to include the recipient's apartment or suite number (if applicable). Naturally, you should use the proper two-letter state abbreviation, and the correct ZIP code—and, when possible, the four-digit ZIP+4 add-on.

TIP Don't know the ZIP code for the address you're shipping to? Look it up at the U.S. Postal Service's ZIP Code Finder at www.usps.com/zip4/.

After you've created the delivery label, place it on the top (not the side) of the box. To avoid confusion, place only one address label on the box. If using a packing slip, place it on the same surface of the box as the address label. Do not place the label over a seam or closure or on top of sealing tape.

TIP To avoid ink smudges and rain smears, place a strip of clear packing tape over the address label.

By the way, if you're shipping via the U.S. Postal Service, you can print labels on your home printer directly from your home computer, using USPS' Click-N-Ship service (http://cns.usps.com). You print a label with prepaid postage; you pay from your computer, using a credit card. Just affix the label to your package and drop it in the mail; no need to visit the post office!

TO INSURE OR NOT INSURE?

If you're shipping a moderately expensive item (over $50, let's say), it might be worth the trouble to offer insurance to the buyer. It's relatively easy to give the buyer the option of buying insurance—or just do it yourself and include the costs in your normal shipping/handling fee.

The U.S. Postal Service charges $1.65 to insure items up to $50, or $2.05 for items between $50 and $100. UPS includes $100 worth of insurance in its basic rates; additional insurance can be purchased for additional cost.

TIP You can also arrange shipping insurance via a third-party firm. For example, U-PIC (www.u-pic.com) provides insurance for packages shipped via the USPS, UPS, FedEx, and other carriers.

SHIPPING INTERNATIONALLY

Packing for international customers shouldn't be any different than for domestic customers—as long as you do it right. Foreign shipments are likely to get even rougher treatment than usual, so make sure the package is packed as securely as possible—with more than enough cushioning to survive the trip to Japan or Europe or wherever it happens to be going.

What *is* different about shipping internationally is the paperwork—and the shipping costs. Make sure you do your homework to find out what it costs to ship to a specific country; you know it's higher than shipping domestically.

As to paperwork, all packages shipping outside U.S. borders must clear customs to enter the destination country—and require the completion of specific customs forms to make the trip. Depending on the type of item you're shipping and the weight of your package, you'll need either Form 2976 (green) or Form 2976-A (white). Both of these forms should be available at your local post office.

Servicing Your Customers

11

When you start selling your crafts online, you're now responsible for something that may be new to you—taking care of your customers. I'm talking basic customer service here, making sure that your customers receive what they order, that they have all their questions answered, that they're informed all through the process, and that they're happy with the way things turned out.

You know you've provided good customer service when you have a happy customer. But how do you make everyone happy?

ANSWERING CUSTOMER QUESTIONS

The more items you sell online, the more likely you'll run into potential buyers who have questions about your crafts. Most online marketplaces let shoppers email sellers with such questions, and if you run your own ecommerce website, you should provide the facility for visitors to email you their questions, too. It's important that you make it easy for potential customers to contact you.

When you receive a question from a potential buyer, you should answer the question promptly, courteously, and accurately. It's in your best interest to make the questioner happy; after all, that person could turn out to be a profitable customer. Remember, you are running a business, and all good businesses go to great lengths to respond appropriately to customer queries.

NOTE Not all crafters are comfortable communicating directly with customers—to which I say, tough. If you don't want to talk to your customers, you shouldn't be selling your crafts, period. Customer communication and satisfaction are part and parcel of running a business—any kind of business. So deal with it!

Potential buyers ask questions because they don't understand something about what you're selling or have some qualms about making a purchase. You need to not only answer the stated question—as thoroughly as possible—but also anticipate any additional questions that customer might have. Your goal, after all, is to sell the item you have listed, so anything you can do to better present the item to buyers will help you make the sale.

What happens if you get a *lot* of questions from shoppers? I have no great advice for you here, other than to just forge ahead. You have to craft each response individually, answering the questions as posed. You may want to batch all the query emails into a bunch, however, and answer them once a day. But you shouldn't worry too much about this; for most sellers, the volume of customer queries will be relatively small and easily manageable.

TIP If you're getting a lot of questions about a particular item, it's a sign that you're not including enough information in your item listing. Consider revising the description to be more descriptive, and possibly shoot additional photos to help clarify any issues.

MANAGING POST-SALE CORRESPONDENCE

Questions from shoppers are only part of your customer service responsibility. As your online crafts business grows, you face a major challenge in managing all the customer correspondence that occurs after a purchase is made. In order, here are the emails that might flow between you and a customer:

- **Purchase confirmation.** This is a simple email thanking the customer for her purchase and detailing the item(s) purchased. This email can also include an estimate of when the item will ship. If the customer paid on checkout, you should also include confirmation of payment. If not…

- **Payment confirmation.** If the customer paid separately from the initial purchase (possible on some online marketplaces) you may need to send out a separate confirmation when payment is received. This is also necessary if the customer paid via personal check or money order; you send this out when the payment arrives in the mail.

- **Shipping confirmation.** You send out this email the day you ship the item to the purchaser. Ideally, this email will include an estimate of the arrival date, the name of the shipping service you used, and the tracking number for this shipment.

- **Thank you.** When all is said and done, it doesn't hurt to send out yet another email thanking the customer for her purchase. You can even use this email to relay additional items you think the customer might be interested in, and encourage future purchases.

That's three, possibly four, outgoing emails on your part. Multiply this by the total number of items you sell, and you can see that email management can a major chore for high-volume sellers.

Now, if your sales volume is sufficiently low, there's no reason you can't handle your necessary correspondence manually, using your normal email program. Just fire up Outlook or Gmail or whatever, type in the text of your message, and click the Send button.

You can automate this process, to some degree, by creating your own form letters. That means creating boilerplate text you use for each of your different customer emails, loading that text into a new message, and then customizing the message with the details of that particular auction. This is a better option than starting from scratch with every sale you make.

TIP Some online marketplaces and website hosting services help you automate the customer communication process. Check with your site of choice to see what email communication features it provides.

HANDLING CUSTOMER COMPLAINTS

Not all sales transactions go smoothly. Maybe the item arrived damaged. Maybe it didn't arrive at all. Maybe it wasn't exactly what the customer envisioned. Maybe the buyer is a loud, complaining, major-league son of a rutabaga.

In any case, if you have a complaining customer, you need to do something about it. Unfortunately, there are really no hard and fast rules for handling post-sale problems. You have to play it by ear and resolve each complaint to the best of your ability.

On the plus side, most people are easy to deal with and just want to be treated fairly. Others, however, won't be satisfied no matter what you offer them. You have to use your own best judgment on how to handle each individual situation.

What are your options when you have a complaining customer? Well, you could just ignore him—not that I really recommend this course of action. If you specified that the merchandise was sold "as-is" or that "all sales are final," you're technically in the clear and don't have to respond to any customer complaints. That's not a good way to run a business, however, as dissatisfied customers don't generate good word of mouth. Besides, you want all your customers to be happy, don't you?

It's far better to try to work something out, if you at all can. If the item never arrived, you can contact the shipping service to put a trace on the shipment. If the item was insured, you can initiate a claim for the lost or damaged item. And if the item doesn't fit or isn't what the customer thought he was buying, you can work out some sort of refund. Even if you're not disposed to offer a full refund, you can perhaps negotiate a lower price or discount with the customer, and then refund the difference—which may be preferable to taking the thing back and losing the entire sale.

TIP Try not to let complaining customers get under your skin. Do your best not to overreact—and definitely don't take the complaint personally. Avoid the temptation to respond with a scathing email and give the customer a piece of your mind. Get up from the computer and go take a walk; blow off some steam before you respond. It's just business, after all.

LISTING YOUR TERMS OF SERVICE

One way to reduce the number of customer complaints is to state very clearly what you do and do not do, right up front in your item listings and, if you have one, on a prominent page on your website. These details are called your terms of service (TOS), and they are the rules that you apply to your sales, the do's and don'ts of how you do business. Think of the TOS as the "fine print" that you want potential customers to be aware of before they make a bid.

Here is a short list of some of the items you might want to include in your TOS:

- **Payment policies**, such as "U.S. funds only," "No personal checks," or "Personal checks take two weeks from date of receipt to clear."

- **Shipping policies**, such as which shipping service(s) you use, how long it generally takes to ship out an order (number of days after the initial sale), your shipping/handling charges (although these may be better placed with the individual item listings), and such.

- **Returns policies**, such as whether or not you accept returns (or if "all sales are final"), how to contact you to return an item, what qualifies for a return, and so forth.

- **Product guarantees and warranties**, if you have them.

- **Contact information**, in case a customer has a question or problem. Email addresses are normal, but customers really appreciate a phone number to call, if you want to divulge that.

Put a short but clear TOS at the bottom of every item listing you run. And if the marketplace lets you create a TOS for your shop or profile, do so. (Etsy, for example, lets you create selling policies for your shop, like the one shown in Figure 11.1.)

A good solid TOS or set of policies may not eliminate *all* customer complaints, but at least you'll make your position known to all potential buyers—before they buy.

GUARANTEEING YOUR MERCHANDISE

You can head off some customer complaints by guaranteeing the craft items you sell. (Alternatively, you can sell all items "as-is"—as long as you clearly indicate this in your item listings.)

Some novice craft sellers might worry that the costs of guaranteeing their merchandise might be prohibitive. This is not the case—if for no other reason than the vast majority of merchandise arrives intact and in good working condition. The number of customers who will actually take you up on a "money back guarantee" will likely be extremely small.

TheArtofChic's Shop Policies

Welcome	We are a new shop here on Etsy and are excited to offer you fun, eclectic handmade or vintage home accessories. See something you like but want a different color? Shoot me an email. We are very flexible and love custom orders.
Payment	Payment Method: Paypal or Money Order
	Terms:
	I try to ship within three business days from the day the order is placed. Therefore, if you need to cancel your order, I will refund your money within three business days or until the item has shipped. Otherwise, all sales are final.
	*Shipping time may vary from item to item and buyer will be notified of any delays.
Shipping	USPS Priority or Parcel Mail
	All breakable items and orders over $50 will be insured.
	Please convo me for all international shipping quotes. Thanks!
Refunds and Exchanges	Please see our payment policies. All sales are final. However, with that said, we never want an unhappy customer. Just send us a message and we will always do our best to make the situation right for everyone.
Additional Policies and FAQs	We love custom orders! Feel free to shoot us an email with any ideas you might have.

FIGURE 11.1

A typical terms of service from an Etsy seller—in the Policies section of the owner's shop.

When a customer is dissatisfied with her purchase and takes you up on your guarantee, you have a couple of options. First, you can offer to refund the purchase price if the item is returned to you. This approach prevents disreputable customers from taking advantage of you by claiming something is bad when it's not; you get to inspect the returned merchandise before you send the refund.

> ✂ **TIP**   You can choose to refund (1) just the purchase price; (2) both the purchase price and the original shipping/handling charge; or (3) the purchase price, the shipping/handling charge, and the customer's costs to ship the item back to you. Make it clear which it is before you ask the customer to return the item.

Second, you can offer a full refund on the item, no questions asked, no further action necessary. With this option, the customer doesn't have to bother with shipping it back to you; this is the way high-class merchants handle their returns. The upside of this method is the extra measure of customer satisfaction; the downside is that you could get taken advantage of, if the customer is so inclined.

You also have to determine just *what* it is that you're guaranteeing. Do you guarantee that the item is in perfect condition? Or that it's simply as described in your item listing? Whatever your guarantee, you're likely to come across the occasional disgruntled customer who feels that the item he received is not as it was described. (Which is another good reason to include a detailed description of the item—and a photograph—in all your item listings.) This situation can quickly deteriorate into an exercise in who said what. It might be best to defuse the situation early by offering some sort of compensatory partial refund, whatever what is stated in your official returns policy.

How long your guarantee lasts is another question. Should you respond to customer complaints 30 days, or 90 days, or even a year after the sale? While a large manufacturer might offer an unconditional one-year guarantee, you probably don't have the same obligation. I'd say that any problems that crop up after the first 30 days shouldn't be your obligation. Most customers will understand and agree.

Whatever guarantee you offer, state it up-front in your item listing or store policies. An official policy is no good if no one knows about it.

Managing Your Inventory

12

One of the challenges of selling online is keeping track of what you have available to sell. In business terms, that means managing your inventory—making sure that what you promote on a given marketplace or website actually exists and can be shipped to customers.

Inventory management doesn't have to be difficult, although there are some issues unique to craft sellers—such as your ability to make more of what you offer and the challenge of selling the same stuff across multiple sites. But those issues are easily dealt with if you're somewhat organized, as you'll soon learn.

HOW TO MANAGE YOUR CRAFT INVENTORY

To sell online, you have to have merchandise available to sell. Now, given that you handcraft everything you have for sale, adding items to your inventory is as simple as making more of what you offer.

That said, can you really offer something for sale if you haven't made it yet? The answer is a firm, "maybe."

BUILD IN ADVANCE OR BUILD TO ORDER?

To me, the ideal situation is to have an item built and ready to go, and then offer it for sale. This way you know if somebody clicks that "buy" button tomorrow, you can grab what's sold and ship it out immediately. That provides for optimal customer satisfaction.

The problem with making something in advance of offering it for sale comes if no one actually buys it. You're out time and materials for a given item that just sits on your shelf, which is less than ideal.

This is why some crafters create listings for crafts they know how to make (and, quite likely have made in the past) but are not yet constructed. When the order from a customer comes in, these crafters get to work and build whatever it was that the customer purchased. It's a build-to-order model, if you're thinking in those terms.

The problem with building after a customer orders is that you may not be able to ship that custom item as fast as you could one that was already made. Now, this depends on a large degree on what type of crafts you sell. If it's a small something you can assemble in an hour or two, and you have all the necessary materials on hand, this model might work very well. If, on the other hand, it takes a week to craft an item—or maybe longer, if you have to order materials—you have the recipe for a dissatisfied customer in your hands.

This last point can be mitigated if you state up-front in your item listing that each item is built to order, and thus it will take X amount of time to fill all orders. Some customers will be willing to wait for a true handcrafted original; others won't, and won't proceed with the purchase.

The build-to-order approach may also be attractive if you offer a given item in different colors or sizes. For example, if you make handcrafted sweaters or dresses, like the seller in Figure 12.1, you can offer a given item in a variety of sizes or colors without necessarily stocking all those sizes in advance. Maybe you have a few of the most common sizes pre-made for immediate shipping, but also offer the item in additional sizes with X days extra shipping. This is a model that works for many clothing sellers.

FIGURE 12.1

This seller offers handmade sundresses in a variety of children's sizes.

In any case, you need to decide whether you're going to build in advance or in response to individual orders. You can then write the shipping details in your item descriptions accordingly.

MAINTAINING ADEQUATE INVENTORY LEVELS

If you do decide to make your crafts in advance, you'll need to put in place some sort of inventory management system to make sure that you always have the items you sell in stock.

To do this, you need to set some sort of minimum quantity for each item you always want to keep on hand. You'll also need to know how long it takes to make each item you sell; this should include any lag time involved in ordering new materials.

Ideally, you'd know how many of a given item you sell in an average month, and use this information to predict when you will run out of stock. You would then schedule to build more of that item at just the right time before the last one is sold. For example, if you know it takes a week to make a given item, you'd arrange to build a new one a week before your last one sells.

Of course, you won't know when exactly you'll sell any given craft item. Unlike commodity goods, which sell in large quantities day in and day out, most craft items sell in a more sporadic fashion, as they strike buyers' fancies. You probably won't be able to predict when a given item will sell.

This means that, in most cases, you'll be making more of a given item only after you sell the last of the previous inventory. This also means you'll be out of stock of that item until you get more built. That's the nature of the craft business.

TRACKING INVENTORY

Now, if you only carry a few handcrafted item in your online store, it's relatively easy to track sales and inventory levels; you probably do so using index cards, if you wish. But if you offer a larger number of items for sale, keeping track of all of them is a bit more challenging.

This is why you should try to automate your inventory management when you start selling online. While most online marketplaces leave inventory management up to you, some ecommerce hosting services provide inventory management as part of their services.

The way automated inventory management works is simple. You enter information about a given product into a spreadsheet, database, or web form. This information typically includes the product name, perhaps a brief description, your item number, your cost, the product's selling price, the current inventory level, and your reorder point or minimum stocking level. This data feeds an inventory database, which tracks the stocking levels for all the products you sell. When an item is purchased by a customer (as noted by the checkout system), the inventory level for that item is reduced accordingly. When the stock reaches the minimum or reorder level, you're notified that you need to make more of that item, which you then should do.

If your hosting provider or online marketplace doesn't provide inventory management functionality, then you'll have to do all this manually—or come up with your own semi-automated solution. Some sellers cope by creating their own inventory management spreadsheet or database, using Microsoft Excel or Access. They have to enter all your sales manually into the spreadsheet or database, but can still use the software to track inventory levels and generate reorder reports.

Bottom line, if you stock a large number of items, you need some sort of inventory management system. The alternative is to risk being out of stock on your best-selling items.

MANAGING INVENTORY ACROSS MULTIPLE MARKETPLACES

Craft selling is interesting in that crafters often offer the same items on multiple marketplaces—on both Etsy and eBay, for example. That doesn't mean you actually have two of those items, one set aside for Etsy customers and the other for eBay customers. No, it often means that you have one of a given item and are offering it to potential customers on two different sites.

> **TIP** You don't have to offer the same goods on different marketplaces. One way to avoid inventory management issues is to offer a distinct mix of items on each site on which you sell, with no overlap at all.

BENEFITS OF OFFERING ITEMS ON MULTIPLE SITES

Why would you want to offer your crafts on more than one marketplace or website? There are a number of reasons, all of which boil down to making more money:

- You can reach more potential customers for the crafts you make. It's simple. You sell on eBay, you reach only eBay customers. You sell on both eBay and Etsy, and you reach customers who frequent both sites. Now, the customer bases of two different marketplaces may have some overlap—that is, some customers may shop on both sites—but in almost all instances, you'll increase the number of potential customers for your products. This increased exposure should result in increased sales for the items you make and sell.

- You can tailor your product mix to the strengths of different marketplaces. We all know that eBay is good for selling some types of items but less good for others. So why not sell eBay-friendly items on eBay and other types of items on another site? There's no reason for you to artificially limit the crafts you make because the single site you sell on isn't friendly to some types of items. Instead, sell some items in one place and other items in another—and play to each channel's strengths.

- It's cost efficient. Just because you sell on two different sites doesn't mean you double your costs. In fact, many of your fixed costs don't change at all if you sell in more than one place. Your rent, utilities, and the like are the same whether you sell on one site or three. You can effectively spread these fixed costs over multiple sites if you go this route.

- It's operationally efficient. While there are some operational challenges for selling on multiple sites, there are also some operational efficiencies to be gained. For example, you only need to shoot one digital photo and write a single description that you can then use in multiple product listings across multiple sites. There's a lot of work you need only do once for multiple marketplaces.

The end result of these advantages is that you should be able to achieve greater sales with not much more effort—which should increase your profits correspondingly.

> **TIP** Avoid the temptation to sell an item at different prices in different marketplaces. Given that your customers are likely to shop more than one website, you should offer identical pricing to the same items sold on different sites.

DRAWBACKS OF OFFERING ITEMS ACROSS MULTIPLE SITES

That said, there are some definite drawbacks to selling a single item across two or more sites. The chief issue is what happens when you sell that item. Assuming it's a unique item, once you sell it to a customer on Etsy, for example, then it's no longer available to be purchased on eBay. The challenge is then removing that listing from eBay before somebody else tries to purchase it—that is, to purchase an item that no longer exists.

This, of course, is an inventory management issue—and one you need to address.

Now, the most inventory-efficient way to manage multiple marketplaces is to create a single pool of inventory for a given item. This works okay under a few conditions. First, all of your marketplaces have to tie into that inventory; when a sale is made in one channel, it has to be reflected in the inventory available for the others. This requires tight inventory management processes, which probably means advanced inventory management software designed for use with multiple channels—definitely not something suited for the occasional craft seller.

Second, you need to have more units on hand than you have outlets. That is, if you sell in two marketplaces, you need to have two or more units on hand at all times—enough to show availability on each site.

Things become problematic if you have fewer units on hand than you have marketplaces. Let's say, for example, that you sell handpainted artwork, where each piece is unique. By definition, you only have one unit on hand for that piece of artwork. The problem comes when you list that piece as "available" on two different websites.

If your inventory management is tight, you should be able it sell the piece on one site and immediately register an "out of stock" situation on the other site. Since not all inventory management systems operate in real time—especially if you manage your inventory by hand—it's more likely that when you sell the piece on site one, it will still show "available" on site two for a period of time—minutes, hours, maybe even days. And if it appears to be in-stock, the possibility exists for a second customer to purchase it—even though it really doesn't exist.

This, then, is the challenge behind managing inventory across multiple marketplaces. Different sellers handle this challenge in different ways.

MULTI-SITE INVENTORY MANAGEMENT SOLUTIONS

One solution is to simply keep as many units on hand as you have marketplaces. If you sell on both Etsy and eBay, you always keep two units of each item on hand. The problem is that, while this approach works well for commodity items, it's not always feasible for one-of-a-kind handmade items.

Another solution is to physically assign inventory units to different channels—that is, to *not* work with pooled inventory. If you sell on three sites, then, you manage three separate inventories. While this helps to keep each marketplace fully stocked, it eliminates one of the beneficial efficiencies of multi-marketplace selling.

Yet another approach is to not sell across multiple sites. You split up the items you sell and offer some on one site and others on another—but never offer the same item on multiple sites. It's a clean approach, if less than efficient.

For most craft sellers, given manageable sales levels, you should be able to handle this situation with tight inventory management. That is, you're probably not going to sell more than one of a given item on any given day. Go ahead and offer your crafts across multiple sites, but when you make a sale on one site, either quickly remove that item listing from the other sites, or quickly make another of that item (if you can). You'll need to keep a close eye on what you're listing and what's selling, but it's probably something you can manage.

> **TIP** If you accidentally sell a one-of-a-kind item twice, you'll have to graciously contact the second buyer and inform her that this item is no longer available. You can then offer a similar item for the same price, or refund the customer's money.

Promoting Your Business with Pinterest

13

Just listing your items for sale doesn't guarantee that anyone will buy them—or even see them. To successfully sell your crafts online, you have to make sure that a lot of potential customers see the items you have for sale. This means promoting your crafts to as many potential customers as possible.

One of the more popular ways to promote your crafts online is a relatively new online social network called Pinterest. This site isn't an online marketplace; you can't sell your goods on the Pinterest site. What Pinterest does, however, is expose your crafts to a wide audience through the social activity of "pinning." The more often your crafts are pinned and repinned on Pinterest, the more traffic you'll drive to your sales listings—no matter which marketplace you use.

GETTING TO KNOW PINTEREST

Pinterest (www.pinterest.com) is a visually-oriented social network that uses the metaphor of "pinning" visual items to a virtual corkboard (called a *pinboard*), and then sharing those items online. It's kind of like a Facebook with pictures only, where people share photos and other images they find interesting with their family and friends. (Figure 13.1 shows the Pinterest main page, filled with "pins" from the site's users.)

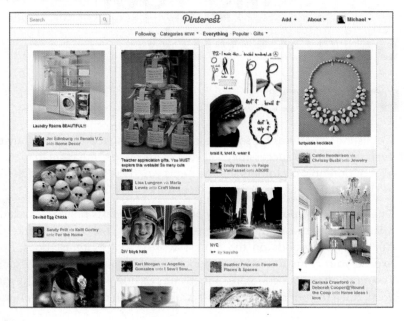

FIGURE 13.1

Tons and tons of "pins" on the Pinterest home page.

As you might have heard, Pinterest is attracting a lot of attention from a lot of people. As of May, 2012, Pinterest had more than 20 million users, up from fewer than a half million less than a year prior. That's a huge growth rate, more than even Facebook had at that point in its development.

More important, people who use Pinterest are really engaged with the site. Users spend an average of 88 minutes per month on the Pinterest site; this compares to 5 minutes per month for Google+ users, 16 minutes/month for LinkedIn users, and 24 minutes/month for Twitter users. The only social media with more engagement are Facebook and Tumblr.

As to who is using Pinterest, it's all about the ladies. Pinterest users are primarily female (58%), mainly between the ages of 24-44 (59%), and typically have incomes between $30,000 and $100,000. That's an attractive demographic—and one that speaks directly to the crafts market.

Why should you, a crafts seller, be interested in Pinterest? It's all in those demographics. Educated females use Pinterest—and that's right in line with who is interested in arts and crafts. You can see the connection by browsing Pinterest and seeing all the pins from the Etsy website; other crafters are already using Pinterest to gain broader exposure for the crafts they have for sale.

When you want to present your crafts to a wide audience of potential buyers, then, Pinterest is as targeted as you get. Plus, it's completely free to use—and who doesn't like free promotion?

USING PINTEREST

After a long public testing phase, Pinterest is now open to the general public. All you have to do is sign up to create your own (free) account.

SIGNING UP FOR A PINTEREST ACCOUNT

To sign up for Pinterest, go to the Pinterest site (www.pinterest.com) and click the red Join Pinterest button. When the next page appears, choose to sign up via either Facebook or Twitter, or by signing up with your own email address. Follow the onscreen directions from there.

NOTE There is no charge to create an account; using Pinterest is completely free. You do, however, need to have a Facebook or Twitter account to sign up for Pinterest.

Once you've created a new Pinterest account, you're prompted to enter some basic information about yourself in order to set up your account. This creates your personal profile on the Pinterest site, so go ahead and enter as much information as you can. You want anyone following you on Pinterest to get to know you and the crafts you create.

HOW PINS WORK

Pinterest is all about pinning images from the web to a user's personal pinboards. Here's how it works.

A person finds an image on a web page that she likes and wants to share. She clicks a "Pin It" button on her web browser's bookmarks bar, or clicks the Add button on the Pinterest site, and the selected image is "pinned" to one of her personal online pinboards.

Figure 13.2 shows a typical pin, which includes the following elements:

- The image that is pinned.

- A short text description from the person who pinned the image.

- The name of the person who pinned the image.

- The name of the person's pinboard to which the image was pinned.

FIGURE 13.2

A typical pin; note the link to the originating website—in this case, the Etsy crafts marketplace.

If others have commented on a pin, their comments appear beneath the pinned image. If comments are present, a Comment box is also displayed; you can comment on the pin by entering your message into this Add a Comment box and then pressing Return.

WHAT HAPPENS WHEN YOU CLICK A PIN

Users can click the various elements of a pin to go to other parts of the Pinterest site, as follows:

- Click the person's name beneath the pinned image to go to the pinner's personal Pinterest page. This page, like the one in Figure 13.3, contains that user's personal profile and picture, as well as all of that user's pinboards.

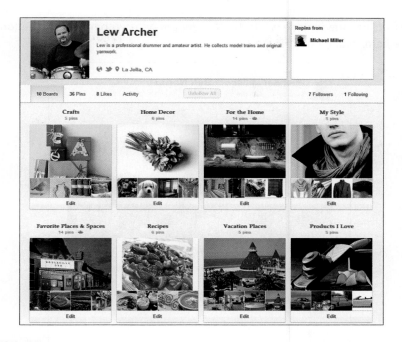

FIGURE 13.3

A user's personal Pinterest page.

■ Click the pinboard's name beneath the pinned image to view the pinner's pinboard to which the image is pinned.

■ Mouse over the pinned image to display buttons that let you repin, like, or comment on a pin, as shown in Figure 13.4.

FIGURE 13.4

Mouse over a pin to repin, like, or comment.

■ Click the pinned image to display a larger pin page with more information about the item, as shown in Figure 13.5.

FIGURE 13.5

Viewing the larger pin page.

> **NOTE** Repinning an item places a copy of that pin on a person's own pinboard. This repinning is the social aspect of the Pinterest social network, and the way that a lot of pins go viral.

The large pin page is the user's link to the original web page for this item. When someone clicks the large pinned image, they're taken to the items original web page. So if it's a pin you've made, clicking that big image takes them to the item listing on the originating marketplace.

UNDERSTANDING PINBOARDS

A Pinterest pinboard is pretty much a traditional cork pinboard; it's where you "pin" items of interest, in a virtual fashion. A user's pinboards, then, become places where she creates and shares collections of those things she likes or finds interesting—including crafts and DIY projects.

Pinterest creates a few default pinboards when a user first signs up, such as Products I Love and My Style. A user can then create as many other pinboards as she likes, organized around her favorite topics and interests. (Figure 13.6 shows a collection of pinboards.)

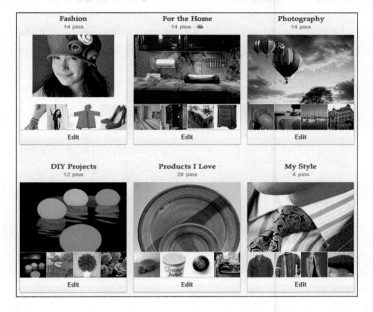

FIGURE 13.6
One user's collection of Pinterest pinboards.

When the user finds an interest item to pin, she determines which of her pinboards to pin it to. Ideally, a pinboard contains items having to do with a specific topic—which can then be shared with other users, or followed by other users.

FOLLOWING OTHER USERS

Key to Pinterest's social interactions is the concept of *following*. When a user finds someone who posts a lot things they happen to like, they can choose to follow that person on Pinterest. When you follow a person, that means that all that person's new pins will display on your own Pinterest home page.

In short, friends who follow a user see the images she pins, and she sees the ones her friends pin. And, in addition to following individual people, users can also follow individual pinboards. This way someone can see new pins about a given topic without having to also see unrelated pins from that person.

Following another Pinterest user is as easy as going to that user's personal Pinterest page and clicking the Follow All button, shown in Figure 13.7. To follow only a given pinboard, go to the user's page and click the Follow button for that particular pinboard.

FIGURE 13.7

Click the Follow All button to follow all of a user's pins.

By the way, Etsy has its own presence on the Pinterest site. Figure 13.8 shows Etsy's profile page, and all of its various pinboards. You can opt to follow all of Etsy's pins or just the pins on a specific pinboard.

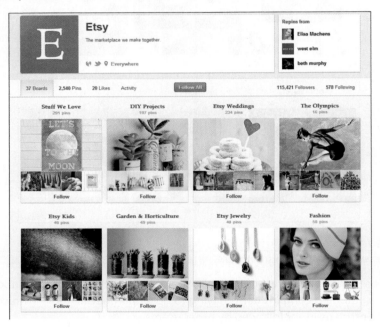

FIGURE 13.8

Etsy's Pinterest profile page.

PINNING YOUR ITEM LISTINGS TO PINTEREST

Using Pinterest for promotion is really just as simple as pinning your craft listings to one or more pinboards, and then encouraging other users to follow your boards and repin your pins. Over time, the word will spread and your listing will get more visitors—and more buyers.

The first step, then, is learning how to pin your crafts to your own Pinterest pinboards. This is really quite easy. All you need is a Pinterest account (it's free, remember) and then you can pin any listing you have on any online marketplace to one of your pinboards.

The simplest (but not necessarily the easiest) way to create a pin is from the Pinterest site. You can also install a Pin It button in your web browser or upload an image to pin, but those all require additional steps.

To pin an item from the Pinterest website, you need to know the address (URL) of the web page you want to pin. This means going to your listing page on Etsy or another website and either copying or writing down the page's URL, found in the Address box of your web browser.

With that URL in hand, log onto the Pinterest site and click Add+ on the Pinterest menu bar. When the Add panel appears, click Add a Pin. Then, when the Add a Pin panel appears, paste or manually enter your listing's URL and click the Find Images button.

The Add a Pin panel now changes to display a slideshow of images found on the selected web page, as shown in Figure 13.9. In the case of an item listing pin, these images should include the multiple photos of the item you have on that site. Click the Next or Prev buttons to cycle through the images until you find the one you want to pin.

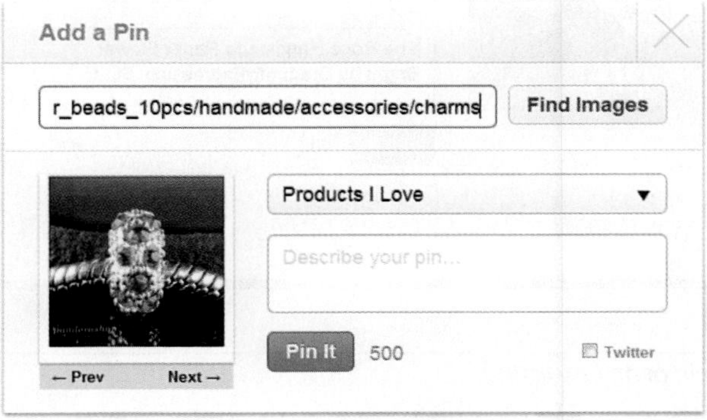

FIGURE 13.9
Pinning an item to Pinterest.

Next, pull down the pinboard list and select the board to which you'd like to pin this image. Enter a short (500 characters or less) text description of or comment on your craft into the Describe Your Pin box; then click the red Pin It button. That's it; your craft listing is now pinned to your selected pinboard, where anyone following your boards or searching for a similar item can see and repin it.

> ✂ **TIP**   It's even easier to pin an item if you install Pinterest's Pin It button in your web browser. For detailed instructions, see www.pinterest.com/about/goodies/.

PINNING AN ETSY LISTING

If you want to pin an Etsy listing to Pinterest, you don't have to go through this entire process. That's because Etsy has added Pin It buttons to all of its listings, like the one shown in Figure 13.10. Pinning a listing is as easy as clicking this Pin It button.

FIGURE 13.10

Click the Pin It button to pin an Etsy item listing.

This opens a Create Pin dialog box, like the one in Figure 13.11. Choose a pinboard and add a text description, as you would normally; then click the Pin It button. The item is now pinned.

FIGURE 13.11

Completing the pin of an Etsy listing.

PINNING AN EBAY LISTING

It's the same thing if you want to pin an eBay item listing. Look for the Pinterest button in the Share section of the listing, shown in Figure 13.12. Click this button; then choose a pinboard and add a text description. It's that easy.

FIGURE 13.12

Click the Pinterest button to pin an eBay item listing.

MAKING YOUR PIN A GIFT ITEM

In addition to its normal pins, Pinterest has a special Gifts section, which users access by clicking the Gifts link on the Pinterest home page. All items in the Gifts section have prices bannered across the top-left corner of each image, as shown in Figure 13.13.

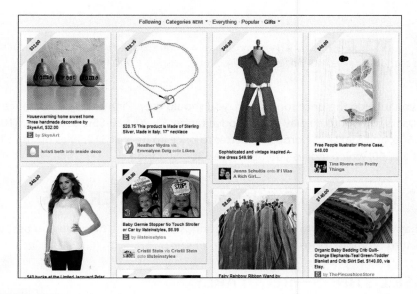

FIGURE 13.13

Pinterest's Gifts section; note the price banners on each pin.

This Gifts section is a great place to showcase craft items you have for sale. To be included in this section, all you have to do is include the item's price in its description, preceded by the dollar sign (or, if you're in the U.K., the pound sign). That's right, just put a dollar sign in your item description and it turns into a gift pin.

When your item is identified as a potential gift, Pinterest automatically places a price banner on the item, as shown in Figure 13.14, and lists it in the Gifts section of the site. The pin itself functions normally; anyone clicking the pin will be taken to that item's listing on the original website.

FIGURE 13.14

A gift pin, complete with price banner.

NOTE The price banner displays anywhere the pin is viewed, not just in the Gifts section. All pins with prices in the description display a price banner.

When you include the price for an item, you should keep Pinterest's default price ranges in mind. Users can opt to display gifts by price range: $1-20, $20-$50, $50-$100, $100-$200, $200-$500, and $500+. It's probably better to price an item at $19.99 to hit the $1-$20 range than at $21.00, which moves you up to the $20-$50 range.

USING PINTEREST TO PROMOTE YOUR CRAFTS

Now that you know how to pin your craft listings to Pinterest, how can you best use Pinterest to promote those crafts you have for sale?

PIN THOSE LISTINGS—REGULARLY

The key to using Pinterest is to actively pin the items you have for sale. Whether you're listing on Etsy, eBay, another marketplace, or your own website, create pins for each new listing you create. Once you get that pin on the Pinterest site, it will be seen by interested users—and their friends, and their friends' friends. (That's the way social networks work—by sharing content posted by ones' online friends.)

NOTE More than 80% of Pinterest's pins are actually repins—items someone else pinned that another user deems worthy of pinning to her own boards.

It's also important to keep pinning; you need to feed the interest of your Pinterest followers. That means creating a new pin each time you create a new item listing, or even relist an item. If you go a week or more without pinning anything, your followers may abandon you. The more (and more regularly) you pin, the more traffic you'll drive to your item listings.

CREATE CUSTOMER-FOCUSED PINBOARDS

Pinterest is all about the pins and the pinboards to which they're pinned. You'll want to create a variety of pinboards that reflect the different types of crafts you offer, and the many ways those crafts can be used by your customers.

When deciding which pinboards to create, then, try to think like your customers. That is, what do your customers expect to see? How do they think of the crafts you create? How do they use those crafts? Let this customer viewpoint influence the types of pinboards you create.

So, for example, if you sell handmade clothing, you might create pinboards for different clothing items—Sweaters, Sundresses, Hats, and the like. Or maybe you create pinboards for different colors—Red, Blue, Green clothing, and the like. Or maybe you create pinboards for different types of customers—Women's Clothing, Men's Clothing, Toddler Clothing, and such. Even better, you could organize your boards around how customers use your products, such as For the Beach, For Formal Occasions, For Around the House, and so forth.

> **TIP** You shouldn't limit your pins to those crafts you have for sale. Many crafters attract new customers by pinning useful and informative links to pages with how-to information, including DIY videos. (Pinterest lets you pin videos as well as pictures.)

And, for each pinboard you create, you should choose an appealing and representative image to serve as that board's main picture. You do this by mousing over a board and clicking the Edit Board Cover button. When the next panel appears, as shown in Figure 13.15, use the arrow buttons to select the board image, and then crop the image as necessary. If you don't do this, each new pin you make becomes the board's cover. By defining a set cover image, that big picture at the top of the board box will always be the one you picked.

FIGURE 13.15

Setting the cover picture for a pinboard.

THINK VISUALLY—BUT DON'T FORGET THE DESCRIPTION

Pinterest is all about the images, which means you need to think visually when you select the image for each item you pin. You want to pin the most attractive images, especially those that "pop" at thumbnail size.

In addition, you need to remember that a pin is more than just a picture; Pinterest also lets you add a short piece of descriptive text. Use this text to tell potential customers about this particular craft item—and to make the pin more searchable. That means incorporating important keywords in the descriptive copy, as well as using #hashtags to encourage further linking and searching.

TIP Pinterest hashtags function just like those on Twitter. A hashtag is essentially a keyword used for searching. Just put the "hash" character (#) in front of a keyword in the description to make it searchable.

LINK PINTEREST TO YOUR WEBSITE OR SHOP

Pinterest lets you add a website link to your personal profile on the site. Use this to link to your primary online store, whether that's your own website or your Etsy shop or eBay Store. Anyone clicking the "world" icon beneath your profile picture is then taken to your main store. (Figure 13.16 shows the web and social networking links beneath a typical Pinterest profile.)

FIGURE 13.16

Web page and social networking links beneath a Pinterest profile.

TIP You should also encourage visitors from your website or marketplace store to follow you on Pinterest. This means embedding a Pinterest Follow button on your company's site, which you can do from www.pinterest.com/about/goodies/. Anyone clicking this button will be taken to your main Pinterest page—and could become a follower and, perhaps, a customer.

LINK PINTEREST TO OTHER SOCIAL NETWORKS

Similarly, you should also link your Pinterest account to your Facebook and Twitter accounts. This cross-posts your Pinterest pins to your other social media, and also displays Facebook and Twitter buttons next to the website button in your profile.

You link Pinterest with your social networks account from your Edit Profile page, shown in Figure 13.17. Just turn "on" the Facebook and Twitter controls and, when prompted, provide your logon IDs and passwords. Pinterest will do the rest.

FIGURE 13.17

Configuring Pinterest to link to your Facebook and Twitter accounts.

Other Ways to Promote Your Business

14

As you learned in the previous chapter, Pinterest is a great (and free!) way to promote the crafts you have for sale. But it's not the only means of promotion you should consider; there are lots of other ways to get the word out there and attract more potential customers.

PROMOTING VIA FACEBOOK

Let's start by considering the Internet's largest social network, Facebook. With more than 800 million users, Facebook (www.facebook.com) can be a powerful promotional tool for your crafts listings.

PROMOTING IN YOUR FACEBOOK NEWS FEED

Assuming that you already have a personal Facebook account, you can post any new craft listings as status updates to your Facebook friends. All you have to do is cut and paste the listing's URL into a new status update, as shown in Figure 14.1, pick the image from the listing you want to include as a thumbnail, and add a little descriptive text. Post the update and all your Facebook friends will read about the new craft listing in their news feeds, as shown in Figure 14.2.

FIGURE 14.1

Creating a Facebook status update for an ArtFire item listing.

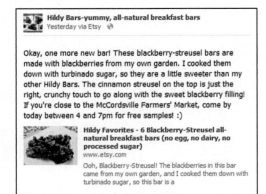

FIGURE 14.2

A Facebook status update promoting a new Etsy listing.

> ✂ **TIP** Depending on where your listing is hosted, you don't even have to do the cut and paste thing. Etsy includes Facebook Like buttons on all their listing pages, and eBay includes a Facebook Share button, both of which perform similarly in creating status updates for your Facebook feed.

CREATING A FACEBOOK BUSINESS PAGE

If you'd rather keep your personal and professional selves separate on the Facebook site, you can create a Facebook Page for your craft business. This page is a lot like a personal profile, but reserved for businesses, products, and public figures, such as entertainers and other celebrities. In your case, you create a Page for your craft business, and use it to post status updates and photos of the new crafts you have for sale.

As you can see in Figure 14.3, a Facebook Page looks a lot like a personal profile page. There's information about the business at the top, along with a profile picture. Below that are individual posts in the standard Facebook timeline format. When friends and customers can "like" your Page, they receive all your status updates in their news feeds.

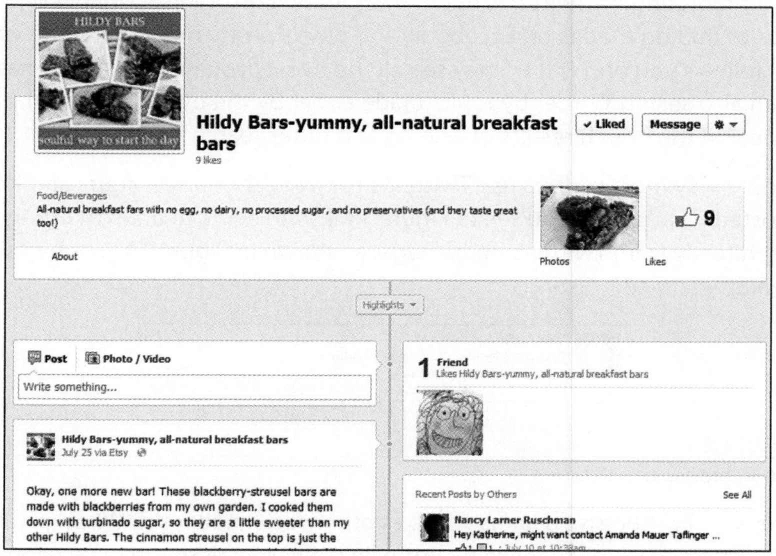

FIGURE 14.3
The Facebook Page for Etsy seller HildyBars (www.facebook.com/HildyBars).

> **NOTE** Like everything on Facebook (save for the deliberate advertising, of course), business Pages are free.

To create a Facebook Page for your business, go to www.facebook.com/pages/ and click the Create Page button. When the Create a Page screen appears, select the category for your Page; I'd recommend either "Local Business or Place" or "Brand or Product." From there, follow the instructions specific to the type of Page you selected. You can then customize the appearance and content of your Page, including adding profile and cover images, editing your timeline activity, highlighting important posts, and so forth. When you're done, just start posting—and getting people to "like" your page.

PROMOTING VIA TWITTER

Facebook may be the largest, but it isn't the only social network out there. To whit, consider Twitter (www.twitter.com), that mini-message service that lets you send out 140-character "tweets" to anyone who's interested enough to follow you.

The key to promoting on Twitter is to get friends and customers to follow you. This is analogous to finding friends on Facebook, and works pretty much the same way. When someone follows you on Twitter, they see all the tweets you make, in their master feed. People can also search Twitter by topic (made easier by the use of hashtags), and tweets often appear in the search results of Google and other search engines.

The standard way most crafters use Twitter is to tweet about new crafts and item listings you've posted. That's what you see in Figure 14.4, with a link to an item listing on Etsy. You can tweet directly from Twitter's home page, as shown in Figure 14.5, or by using the Twitter buttons in Etsy and eBay listings.

FIGURE 14.4

A tweet promoting a craft listing.

As you can see, Twitter isn't near as visual as other social networks. When you tweet a link to an item listing, that's all that's there—the link, plus any descriptive text you add. You can, however, manually attach a picture to a tweet, using the camera icon in the Compose New Tweet box. By default, the photo appears only as a link within the tweet, although viewers can click the View Photo link to view the tweet with the photo embedded, as shown in Figure 14.6.

FIGURE 14.5

Tweeting from Twitter's home page.

FIGURE 14.6

A tweet with an embedded image.

TIP Given the length of most listing URLs and Twitter's strict 140-character limit, you may want to use a URL shortening service, such as bit.ly, to convert the listing's long URL into a much shorter one.

You can tweet about the same things you post about on Facebook. That means new crafts you're working on, new item listings on Etsy and other sites, even craft tips and advice you might have for your followers. Twitter followers tend to expect more frequent updates than do users of other social networks, so you need to keep the tweets coming!

PROMOTING ON ETSY

If you're an Etsy seller, there are several promotional avenues you can use within the Etsy site itself. Let's look at a few of them.

ETSY COUPON CODES

When you want to spur sales of one or more of the items you have listed on Etsy, you can promote them via online coupon codes. You can create coupon codes that offer customers either a percent discount off the normal price or free shipping. Any customer making a purchase enters the coupon code during the checkout process, thus redeeming the virtual coupon and getting the discount or free shipping.

> **NOTE** The percent discount coupon applies to the customer's entire order in your Etsy shop. It does not apply to shipping costs, only to the total item cost.

To create a coupon code for your shop, go to your shop page and click Coupon Codes in the sidebar, in the Promote section. On the next page, click the Create New Coupon button; then create your own custom coupon code and select the type of coupon (Percent Discount of Free Shipping) from the drop-down menu. Set the status to Active when you want the coupon to go live, and then click the Add Coupon button to get things underway.

> **TIP** Your coupon code must be between 5 and 20 alphanumeric characters. Try to create an easily-remembered code, such as JUNEPROMO or something similar.

Naturally, you want to mention the coupon code in your item listings, such as the one in Figure 14.7. You should also promote the code via other means, including Facebook and Twitter posts. The more people you let know about your promotion, the more business it will create.

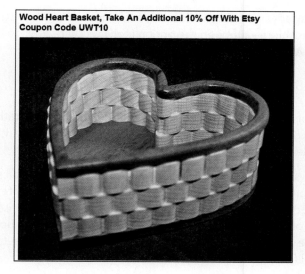

FIGURE 14.7

A listing with 10% off coupon code.

ETSY SEARCH ADS

You can also promote your listings on the Etsy site with Etsy Search Ads. These are the "Sponsored" listings, like the ones in Figure 14.8, that appear at the top of a search results page when someone searches for a particular keyword on the Etsy site.

FIGURE 14.8

Sponsored listings (paid ads, in other words) that appear on Etsy search results pages.

Etsy's sells its Search Ads on a CPM, or cost per impression, basis. That is, you pay about $1 for each 1,000 impressions or times the ad is displayed. You select which keywords you want your ad displayed for, as well as your weekly advertising budget. (You have to spend a minimum of $5 per week.) The more you budget, the more your ad is displayed, and the more likely it is someone will click through to your advertised listing. Of course, the more you budget, the more money you spend, so there's that.

To be honest, Etsy advertising is feasible only for larger sellers. Most Etsy sellers do not advertise in this fashion—although the option is always there. Just go to your shop page and click Search Ads in the sidebar.

ETSY ON SALE

The next batch of Etsy promotional activities aren't run by Etsy, but rather by various third parties. First up is one called Etsy on Sale which, as the name implies, helps you put your Etsy items on sale—and promotes them as such.

Figure 14.9 shows the Etsy on Sale site (www.etsyonsale.com), with all sorts of on-sale listings, searchable and browsable by category. The site lets you create all sorts of sales events for your Etsy listings; the discounts appear in the listings themselves, and the listings appear not only on the Etsy site but also on the Etsy on Sale site. It's not a free service (you have to purchase "credits" in advance, and each sales event costs a set number of credits), but it does simplify the promotional process.

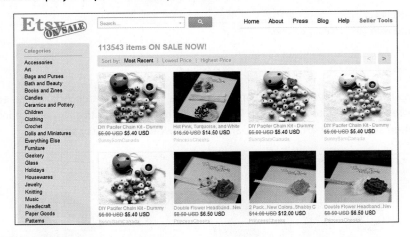

FIGURE 14.9

Items on sale at Etsy on Sale.

PROMOTING IN AN ONLINE CRAFTS MALL

Whether you have an Etsy shop or your own ecommerce website, you can promote your online store in various third-party online crafts malls. These are websites that display and link to crafters' own online storefronts—very much like having your own physical storefront in a traditional crafts mall.

Some of these crafts malls let you create your own virtual storefronts, while others simply link to your existing online shop. Some are free, most cost a small monthly fee. And all help to drive new customers to your Etsy or other online shop.

If you're interested in having this type of presence, check out these major online crafts malls:

- Crafter Marketplace (www.craftermarketplace.com)

- CraftMall (www.craftmall.net)

- Handmade Spark (www.handmadespark.com)

- Jewelry Artist Direct (www.jewelryartistdirect.com), shown in Figure 14.10

- Lilly's Craft Stores Mall (www.lillysplace.net)

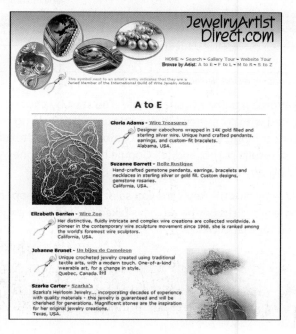

FIGURE 14.10

Some of the stores in the Jewelry Artist Direct crafts mall.

PROMOTING WITH GOOGLE ADWORDS

Finally, if you're a high-volume seller with your own website or Etsy shop, you may want to take the plunge into full-scale online advertising. The most popular online advertising program is Google AdWords, which places text ads on Google's search results pages, like the ones in Figure 14.11; each ad is tied to a specific keyword the user is searching for.

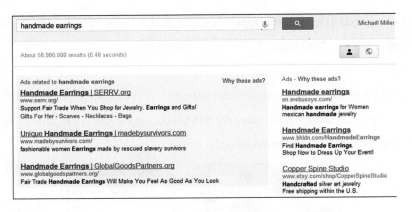

FIGURE 14.11

AdWords PPC text ads on a Google search results page.

Advertising on AdWords is actually quite simple. You start by choosing the keywords you want to be associated with. You then bid the amount you're willing to pay for each payment, typically in the 10-cent range or so. Then you compose the short text ad you want displayed on matching search results pages, and tell Google how much money you want to spend each day. (That's your daily advertising budget.)

When someone searches for the keyword you selected, your ad appears on that search results page. If someone clicks on the ad, he is taken to your web page or online store, and Google charges you for that click.

> **NOTE** AdWords is a form of pay per click or PPC advertising. You only pay when your ad is clicked, not when it's displayed.

You can launch an AdWords campaign with a budget as small as a dollar per day, although larger budgets will get you a lot more exposure. You can advertise your store as a whole or specific items in your store. You choose the link that appears in your ad, along with the ad's text.

As I said, online advertising, such as that offered by Google AdWords, is probably only for larger sellers. The expense is definitely more than most occasional sellers are willing to—or should—spend.

> **NOTE** Learn more about Google AdWords in my companion book, *Using Google AdWords and AdSense* (Michael Miller, Que Publishing, 2010).

Measuring Your 15
Success

Once you get a little online selling under your belt, it's time to start measuring your performance. Are your item listings drawing enough traffic? Are you generating enough sales? And are those sales being done profitably?

Measuring your performance is all about identifying the key metrics and determining whether or not you're performing as desired. That means learning some business basics—and then looking dispassionately at the results.

MEASURING TRAFFIC

Let's start by looking at how many people actually see your craft listings. This requires the employment of something called *web analytics*, or the measurement of web page visitors and views.

UNDERSTANDING WEB ANALYTICS

Web analytics help you measure and analyze traffic to a given web page. There are all sorts of metrics you can track, and if you ran your own big-time website you probably would, but for most craft sellers, only a few metrics are of interest. In particular, here's what you should be looking at:

- **Click.** A single instance of a visitor clicking a link from one page to another. Typically used when measuring ad performance, especially those you pay for on a per-click basis.

- **Click through rate (CTR).** The percentage of people who view an item and then click it. Calculated by dividing the number of clicks by the number of impressions. Also used for measuring PPC ad performance.

- **Impressions.** A single display of an advertisement on a web page.

- **Pageview.** Sometimes just called a *view*, this is simply the display of a given web page. One visitor looking at a single page on your site or in your shop, such as an item listing page, generates one pageview.

- **Visitor.** A person who views the pages on a website—that is, someone who visits your site or shop.

That doesn't seem too difficult. When you want to measure how many people saw an item listing—that is, your listing *traffic*— you track either the number of visitors to that listing or the number of pageviews the listing generated. When you want to measure the performance of any advertising you've purchased, measure clicks, impressions, and the click through rate.

> **NOTE** The number of visitors won't always equal the number of pageviews, as a given visitor can view a page more than once.

TRACKING ETSY TRAFFIC

Now that you know what you should be tracking, how do you track it?

If you have an Etsy shop, you can view basic traffic metrics with the Shop Stats tool. Shop Stats displays views (and other metrics) for your shop in total, or for any selected listing. As you can see in Figure 15.1, you see the total number of views for a given time period, as well as views per day over that time period in the graph below.

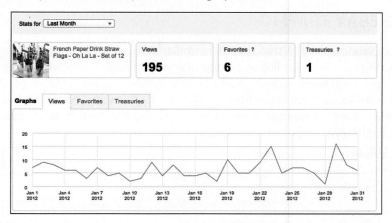

FIGURE 15.1

Tracking views for an Etsy listing with the Shop Stats tool.

If you want more detailed traffic stats, you can use the Etsy Web Analytics tool. This is actually a utility that ties your Etsy shop to another tool, called Google Analytics. We'll talk about Google Analytics in a few pages, but for now know that it's a service, provided by Google, that tracks all sorts of traffic-related metrics. Etsy simply ties it into its shop pages, to measure the visitors and pageviews and so on that your item listing pages receive.

> **NOTE** To use Etsy Web Analytics, you must first have a Google Analytics account and then tie that into your Etsy account, which you do from the Your Account page, in the Shop Settings > Options section.

Once everything is properly configured, you can view all sorts of key metrics, including number of visits, visitors, pageviews, and the like—just what you need to determine how many people are actually viewing your listings.

Whichever tool you use, it's the views/pageviews metric that matters. What can this data tell you? Lots, really. Here are two possible scenarios:

■ If the number of views or visitors is low, your listing isn't being noticed. (Or is being ignored, which isn't quite the same thing.) And if no one's viewing your listing, there's no one there to buy it, and sales will be low.

■ If you have a high number of visitors or views but still have low sales, there's something wrong with your listing. Either your craft is somehow unappealing or your price is too high. You'll need to take some sort of action to convert those views into purchases.

TRACKING EBAY TRAFFIC

If you have listings on eBay, that site offers similar tools for tracking traffic to your listings. When you click the My eBay link at the top of any eBay page, you open the My eBay utility, which is where you keep track of all your eBay activity. Go to the All Selling or Active Selling tabs and you'll see all your active listings. (Figure 15.2 shows the All Selling tab.) For each listing, eBay shows the number of views, watchers, and (for auction items) bids. It's not fancy analytics, but it gives you what you need.

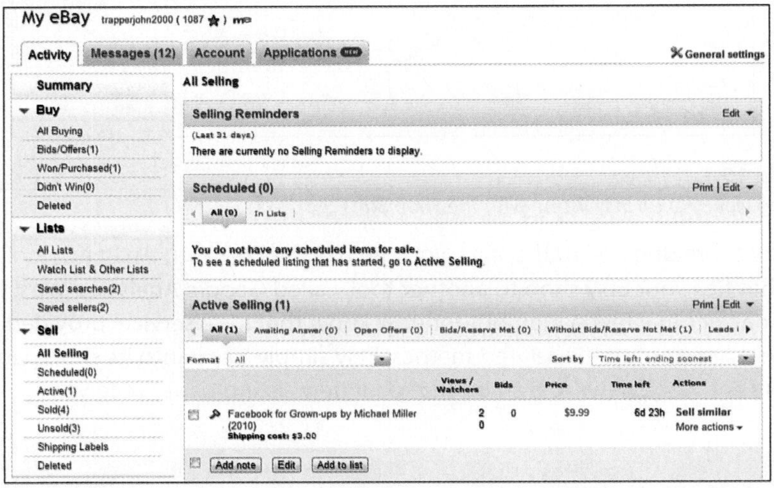

FIGURE 15.2

Tracking views with My eBay.

TRACKING TRAFFIC ON YOUR OWN SITE

If you have your own ecommerce website, your website hosting service might offer its own web analytics tool. If it does, and if it's free, use it.

If you want additional analytics, I recommend you check out Google Analytics (www.google.com/analytics/). This is a free tool, offered by Google, that tracks traffic to any website, using all manner of standard and custom reports.

NOTE Learn more about Google Analytics in my companion book, *Sams Teach Yourself Google Analytics in 10 Minutes* (Michael Miller, Sams Publishing, 2010).

As you can see in Figure 15.3, the Visitor's Overview report provides a wealth of information about visitors to your site. You can track visits, unique visitors, pageviews, pages per visit, average visit duration, bounce rate (what percent of visitors leave your site without doing anything), and percent of new visitors, over any given period of time. And that's just the basic stuff; there's lots more where that came from. Google Analytics is a data junkie's delight, which makes it a very useful tool for tracking the performance of your site. (And remember—it's free!)

FIGURE 15.3
Tracking site visitors with Google Analytics.

MEASURING SALES

Seeing how many people view your item listings is useful, but ultimately what's important is how many of those people actually buy something. That means tracking the sales you make, in terms of both number of sales and revenues generated.

UNDERSTANDING SALES AND REVENUES

In general, tracking sales is fairly straightforward. You can track several sales-related metrics:

- **Units sold.** This is simply the number of units sold, not the dollars associated with those units. So if you sold five of a given item, you sold five units.

- **Transactions.** This is the number of unique transactions you made. Since a single customer can purchase more than one unit per transaction, the number of units sold will not always equal the number of transactions made.

> **TIP** When you know the total number units sold and the number of transactions generated, you can then calculate how many units per transaction you averaged.

- **Revenues.** This is the monetary aspect of things—how many dollars you took in from your sales. For example, if you sold four units at $5 apiece, you generated $20 in revenues.

> **NOTE** You should probably look at your revenues without shipping/handling charges and taxes added. That is, look at revenues from pure item sales.

TRACKING ETSY SALES

If you're selling on Etsy, you can track your sales using the Shop Stats tool. You can view sales either daily or monthly, or for a specific time period. As you can see in Figure 15.4, this tool displays both the number of orders received and revenue generated for the selected time period. You can also choose to graph orders and revenue over that time period.

FIGURE 15.4

Tracking Etsy orders and revenues with the Shop Stats tool.

TRACKING EBAY SALES

On eBay, you track your sales from My eBay. Select the Sold tab (in the Sell section) to view all the sales you've recently made.

If you have an eBay Store, you have access to more detailed reporting. Sales Reports Plus, shown in Figure 15.5, lets you see your total sales, number and percentage of successful items, average sales price per item, sales by category and format, and other important metrics. This is the way to go, very easy and comprehensive reporting, and as good a reason as any to open an eBay Store.

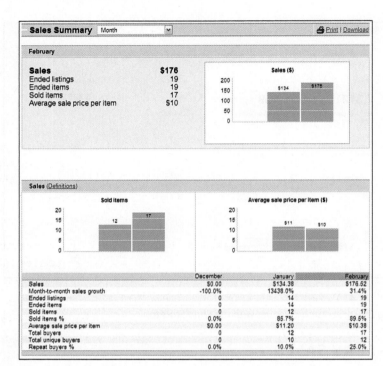

FIGURE 15.5

Tracking eBay Store sales with Sales Reports Plus.

MEASURING PROFITS

Revenues are great—that's cash on hand, at least after you deposit the funds from your payment processing service. But it's not all cash you can spend, because you have expenses to pay. You have to subtract all your expenses from your revenues to find your profit—how much money you're *really* making.

Bottom line, you need to be interested in your bottom line—that is, the net profits you generate. Now, we covered a lot of this territory back in Chapter 2, "Setting the Right Price," so I won't repeat it all here. But in general, you need to measure both your gross profit per item and net profit for your entire business. I'll explain what I mean.

CALCULATING GROSS PROFIT PER ITEM

There are various ways to define and calculate profit, but we're going to keep it simple here. We'll start by looking at how much money you really make for each item you sell—what we call the *gross profit per item*.

Calculating your gross profit is fairly easy, at least in concept. All you have to do is take the selling price of an item and subtract all the costs associated with that item. What's left over is your gross profit for that item. Here's the basic formula:

Gross profit = Selling price – item costs

This simple formula needs a bit of explanation.

First, the selling price is just that—the actual price for which the item sold. If you listed something at $20 but gave a 10% discount, the customer actually paid $18, and that $18 is your selling price. The selling price does *not* include taxes or any shipping/handling fees you add on top. It's just the final price of the item, as paid by the customer.

Item costs can and do include a lot of things. You need to include all of the following:

- **Cost of materials.** That is, the cost of all the component parts of the craft. For example, if you make gift baskets, you'd include the cost of the baskets and all the items you put inside. If you make beaded bracelets, you'd include the cost of the beads and the bracelet string. Don't leave anything out.

- **Cost of labor.** If you assemble your crafts yourself, this is *your* cost. Figure out how much you should be paid, on an hourly basis, and multiply that by the number of hours you work to create that craft. Don't undersell your value; you should probably "pay" yourself more than minimum wage. For example, if you say your time is worth $10 an hour and a given craft took two hours of your time to build, that's $20 in labor costs you need to assign.

- **Listing fees.** If you're listing in an online marketplace, such as Etsy or eBay, that charges a set fee to list an item, you need to throw that into your item cost.

- **Selling fees.** If you're selling in an online marketplace that charges a selling fee or transaction fee or final value fee or sales commission (all phrases that mean the same thing), calculate that cost and include it in the item cost. For example, Etsy charges a transaction fee of 3.5% of the final selling price. If you sell a $20 item, that transaction fee is 3.5% of $20, or $0.70.

> **NOTE** Selling fees or commissions are typically calculated on the selling price of the item only, without adding taxes or shipping/handling fees.

- **Payment processing fees.** If a customer pays via PayPal or Google Checkout or some similar online payment service, you have to include the fees charged by that service in your item cost. For example, PayPal charges 2.9% of the total transaction price, plus a flat $0.30 per transaction. If you sold a $20 item with $6 shipping (total transaction price: $26), you owe PayPal $0.75 plus $0.30, or a total of $1.05 that needs to be included in your item cost.

> **NOTE** Unlike selling fees, payment processing fees are typically charged for the entire value of the transaction—the total amount the customer pays, including tax and shipping/handling.

- **Packaging costs.** We're not talking shipping costs here, which get passed on to the customer via your shipping/handling fees, but rather the cost of those materials you use to pack the item—box or envelope, bubble wrap, Styrofoam peanuts, and so forth.

Add all those costs together to calculate your total item cost, as follows:

Item cost = Cost of materials + cost of labor + listing fees + selling fees + payment processing fees+ cost of packaging

It's this number you subtract from the selling price to calculate the gross profit for an individual item. Assuming that the number is positive, you've made money (generated a profit) on that item, and not sold the item at a loss.

You can then calculate your *profit margin* for an item by dividing your gross profit by the selling price, as follows:

Profit margin = Gross profit / selling price

For example, if you sold an item for $20 and had item costs of $12, you generated an $8 gross profit. Divide that $8 by the $20 selling price ($8/$20) and you discover your gross profit margin of 40%.

> **TIP** What's a good profit margin for an item? Every person and business has different criteria, but I'd say you should strive for a minimum 40% average profit margin, with something in the 60%–75% range being more acceptable.

CALCULATING NET PROFIT FOR YOUR BUSINESS

Your gross profit per item tells you how much money you're making on each individual item you sell. But that doesn't describe the profit for your total business, as you have additional fixed expenses that aren't assigned to individual items. I'm talking about the costs of any tools or machinery you use to assemble multiple items, your rent and utilities, any subscription fees you pay to online marketplace sites or web hosting services, and so forth. You need to figure out these fixed costs before you attempt to calculate how profitable your total business is.

NOTE A fixed cost is one that cannot be assigned to a specific item you sell, but rather is spread out over your entire business. A fixed cost must be paid whether you sell one item or a hundred.

Once you know all your fixed costs, you can calculate the net profit of your entire business as follows:

Net profit = Gross profit – fixed expenses

That is, you take the total gross profit from all the items you've sold in a given period and subtract all your fixed expenses from that same period. What you have left over—assuming there is anything left over—is your net profit. If you end up with a negative number—that is, if your fixed expenses are higher than your gross profit—then your business is losing money, which is not a good thing.

TIP If all these numbers make your head spin, and if your sales are high enough, you should consider hiring an account to handle your business finances for you. You can also use an accounting program such as QuickBooks to manage your business accounting, if you're so inclined.

HOW DO YOU DEFINE SUCCESS?

You can do all the tracking and analysis and calculations and come up with a bottom line number, but what does it all mean? How do you know if your business is really successful?

Unless you're running a charity, I'd say the first measurement of success is profitability. That is, if your business is not generating a net profit—i.e., you're losing money—then you're not successful. You can't lose a dollar on every sale and make it up in volume; if you're losing money overall, why spend the time and effort to keep doing it?

The next question, then, is how much profit is enough? There's no universal answer to that one; you have to determine for yourself how much profit makes the time you spend worthwhile. If all you do is make a few bucks a month, but you don't spend much time doing it, that might be enough for you. If, on the other hand, you put in a full forty hours a week but only end up with a hundred dollars of profit for your work, then you can probably spend your time more profitably elsewhere.

You also need to consider just how many items you're moving, on average, and the amount of time you have to put into the crafting and selling effort. If this is just a hobby for you and you don't put too much time into it, you may be satisfied moving a few units a month. If, on the other hand, you want or need to make this your full-time job, then you need to sell enough items to make the numbers pay out. So your own goals factor into the success equation.

At the end of the day, you need to be happy with what you're doing and how you're doing it. There's undeniable satisfaction in taking part in the online crafts community and getting to know other crafters and craft lovers, and you can't quantify that. You have to take into account the entire experience, not just the profit you make, and decide whether you're successful at selling your crafts online.

I'm betting you'll be a success.

INDEX

A

abbreviations in titles, 35-36
accessories in photos, 56-57
accounts, signing up
  eBay, 120
  Etsy, 98-99
  Pinterest, 189
acronyms in titles, 35-36
advertising
  in Etsy, 96, 209-210
  Google AdWords, 211-212
AdWords, promotion with, 211-212
angles for product photos, 55
annual fees, Yessy, 76
answering customer questions, 172
Artbreak, 66
ArtFire, 66-67
Artful Home, 68

Artist Rising, 69
Artspan, 69-70
auction listings on eBay, 114-115
  adding Buy It Now option, 123
  creating, 121-123
auction sites, 7
automated customer service, 143
automated inventory management, 182

B

background for photos
  color of, 52
  selecting, 48-49
benefits, features versus, 39-40
best-selling items, 10-11
billing from Etsy, 98
BIN option. *See* Buy It Now option
blocking buyers on eBay, 132

Bonanza, 70-71
Bonanzle, 70
bounced checks, 150
boxes
    envelopes versus, 164
    how to pack, 165-166
brightness, correcting in
        photos, 60
business plans
    for full-time sellers, 15
    for growing sellers, 14
    importance of, 12
    for occasional sellers, 13-14
    parts of, 17-18
    questions to ask, 15-17
    reviewing, 20
    talking through, 18-19
    what to include, 12-13
    writing, 20
Buy It Now option on eBay,
        115-116, 123
buyer feedback ratings on
        eBay, 132

C

calculating. *See also* measuring
    costs, 23-25
        what to include, 221-222
    profit, 29, 220-223
    profit margin, 222
    selling price, 26-28
    shipping and handling fees,
        162-163
cameras. *See* digital cameras
capital letters
    in descriptions, 40
    in titles, 35
cards, packing, 166
cash on delivery (C.O.D.)
        payments, 149
cash payments, 149
cashier's checks, 151

categories
    on eBay, 130
    on Etsy, 93-94
centering products in
        photos, 54
channel strategy (in business
        plan), 18
check payments, 107, 150
Checkout by Amazon, 155-156
checkout systems, 135, 142
clear glass, photos of, 57
click through rate (CTR), 214
clicking pins, 190-192
clicks, defined, 214
clothing
    packing, 166
    photos of, 58-59
C.O.D. payments, 149
color
    of background for photos, 52
    correcting in photos, 60
colored fabrics, infrared light
        on, 58
commissions. *See* selling fees
communicating with customers.
        See customer service
complaints, handling, 174
    guaranteeing merchandise,
        175-177
    listing terms of service,
        175-176
confirmation email messages,
        managing, 173
contrast, correcting in
        photos, 60
cost of goods sold, 24
cost per impression (CPM), 209
costs. *See also* fees
    calculating, 23-25
        what to include, 221-222
    ecommerce hosting services,
        144-146
    ecommerce websites, 137-138
    four times cost formula, 26-27

coupon codes in Etsy, 208-209
cover images
    on Etsy, 108-109
    for pinboards, 199
CPM (cost per impression), 209
Craft Count website, 22
craft-focused shopping sites, 6
Craft is Art, 70
craft sales
    best-selling items, 10-11
    business plans. *See* business
        plans
    eBay. *See* eBay
    Etsy. *See* Etsy
    item listings. *See* item listings
    online venues for, 6-8
    selling price. *See* selling price
    what to avoid selling online,
        8-10
    where to sell, 6-8, 63
        comparison of sites, 83-84
        dedicated online craft mar-
            ketplaces, 64-77
        Etsy versus eBay, 86-88
        factors to consider, 84-86
        general online marketplaces,
            78-82
        multiple sites, 89, 183-185
        personal website, 88-89. *See
            also* ecommerce websites
Crafter Marketplace, 211
CraftMall, 211
crafts malls, promotion with,
        210-211
Craigslist, 79-80
credit card payments, 151-152
Crobbies, 71-72
cropping photos, 61
CTR (click through rate), 214
cushioning material for packing
        boxes, 165-166
custom made, premade versus,
        180-181

customer communications management, 135
customer-focused pinboards, 198-199
customer reviews, 135
customer service
  answering questions, 172
  automated, 143
  complaints, handling, 174-177
  confirmation email messages, managing, 173
customizing
  eBay Store, 128
  your Etsy shop, 101-102

D

deactivating item listings on Etsy, 105
dedicated online craft market-places, 64
  Artbreak, 66
  ArtFire, 66-67
  Artful Home, 68
  Artist Rising, 69
  Artspan, 69-70
  Bonanza, 70-71
  Craft is Art, 70
  Crobbies, 71-72
  Etsy, 64-66. See also Etsy
  Funky Finds, 72
  Handmade Artists Shop, 73
  Handmade Catalog, 74
  Hyena Cart, 74
  Made It Myself, 75
  ShopHandmade, 76
  Yessy, 76
  Zibbet, 77
defining success, 223-224
delivery labels, creating, 168-169
demographics of Pinterest, 188

descriptions
  in item listings, 36-40
  in Pinterest, 200
design (of ecommerce website) fees, 137
details in item descriptions, 37-39
DHL, 162
digital cameras, selecting, 44-45
direct checkout on Etsy, 106
discounts, setting selling price, 26-27
domain name registration, 134, 137

E

eBay, 7
  account signup, 120
  auction listings, 121-123
  Etsy versus, 66, 86-88
  explained, 78-79, 112-114
  fees, 117-119
  fixed-price listings, creating, 124
  managing sales, 129
  measuring sales, 219-220
  measuring traffic, 216
  payment methods, 129
  pinning listings from, 196
  pros and cons for crafters, 113-114
  selling methods, 114-117
  selling via personal website versus, 140-141
  Store listings, 125-128
  tips for, 130-132
  tracking sales, 22
  types of sellers, 113
ecommerce websites
  benefits of, 138
  components of, 134-136
  costs of, 137-138

  disadvantages of, 139-140
  hosting services, selecting, 141-146
  measuring traffic, 216-217
  methods of building, 136-137
  selling on, 88-89
  selling via Etsy and eBay versus, 140-141
eCRATER, 80-81
edible items, legal issues, 11
editing
  item listings on Etsy, 105
  photos, 51, 60-61
email addresses, Etsy account signup, 99
envelopes, boxes versus, 164
equipment for photos, 44
  backgrounds, 48-49
  digital camera, 44-45
  external lighting, 46-48
  light tent, 49-50
  photo editing software, 51
  tripod, 46
Etsy, 6
  account signup, 98-99
  appearance of item listings, 94-96
  cover images, 108-109
  creating your shop, 100
  customizing your shop, 101-102
  eBay versus, 66, 86-88
  explained, 64-66, 92
  fees, 96-98
  item categories, 93-94
  item listings, 102-105
  managing sales, 107-108
  measuring sales, 218-219
  measuring traffic, 215-216
  payment methods, 105-107
  pinning listings from, 196
  on Pinterest, following, 194

promotion with, 208-210
selling via personal website versus, 140-141
tips for making money, 108-110
tracking sales, 22
Etsy on Sale website, 27, 210
Etsy Web Analytics tool, 215
Express Mail, 160
external lighting
  for photos, 52-53
  selecting, 46-48

F

Facebook
  Etsy account signup, 98
  linking to Pinterest, 201
  promotion with, 204-206
Facebook Pages, creating, 205-206
features, benefits versus, 39-40
FedEx, 161
FedEx Office, 162
feedback ratings
  on eBay, 132
  on Etsy, 110
fees. See also specific types of fees
  bounced checks, 150
  comparison of sites, 83-84
  considering when selecting sites, 85-86
  Craigslist, 80
  for credit card payments, 152
  for dedicated online craft marketplaces, 64
  ecommerce hosting services, 144-146
  ecommerce websites, 137-138
  eCRATER, 81
  Etsy versus eBay, 87
  insurance for shipped items, 169

PayPal versus Etsy, 107
ShopHandmade, 76
site hosting services, 137, 141
types of, 221-222
final value fees. See selling fees
First Class Mail, 160
fixed costs, 25, 223
fixed price listings on eBay, 116, 124
flat fees for shipping and handling, 163
flat items, scanning, 60
Follow button (Pinterest), installing, 200
following on Pinterest, 193-194
food, legal issues, 11
formatting item descriptions on eBay, 130-132
four times cost formula (calculating selling price), 26-27
fragile items, selling online, 9
framed artwork, packing, 166
framing products in photos, 54
full-time sellers, business plans for, 15
Funky Finds, 72

G

general online marketplaces, 78-82
gift items on Pinterest, 196-198
glare, avoiding, 56
glass
  opaque glass, photos of, 58
  packing, 166
  translucent glass, photos of, 57
goals section (in business plan), 18
Google AdWords, promotion with, 211-212
Google Analytics, 215-216

Google Checkout, 154-155
gross profit, calculating, 29, 220-222
growing sellers, business plans for, 14
guaranteeing merchandise, 175-177

H

HammerTap website, 22
handling charges, calculating, 162-163
Handmade Artists Shop, 73
Handmade Catalog, 74
Handmade Spark, 211
hashtags in Pinterest, 200
home pages, 134
hosting services, selecting, 141-146
The Hutch with Mutch website, 8
Hyena Cart, 74

I

images, cover images for pinboards, 199. See also photos
impressions, defined, 214
increasing feedback rating on Etsy, 110
infrared light on colored fabrics, 58
insertion fees. See listing fees
installing
  Pin It button, 195
  Pinterest Follow button, 200
insurance for shipped items, 169
international shipping, 169
inventory management, 135, 142
  across multiple sites, 182, 185
  automated systems, 182

maintaining levels, 181-182
premade versus custom made,
190-181
invitations (Pinterest), requesting, 189
item categories on Etsy, 93-94
item descriptions on eBay,
130-132
item listings
eBay
auction listings, creating,
121-123
Buy It Now option,
adding, 123
fixed-price listings,
creating, 124
selling methods,
selecting, 117
Etsy
appearance of, 94-96
creating, 102-104
deactivating, 105
editing, 105
number of, 109
renewing, 105
managing, 135
pinning on Pinterest, 194-196
selecting hosting services, 142
writing, 31
descriptions, 36-40
personal style in, 40-41
photos in, 41. *See also*
photos
titles, 32-36

J

jars, packing, 167
jewelry
models for, 60
packing, 167
photos of, 58
Jewelry Artist Direct, 211
JPG file format, 60
juried marketplace, 68

K

keywords, 33. *See also* tags

L

labels, creating shipping labels,
168-169
labor costs
calculating, 24
defined, 221
legal issues
edible items, 11
what to avoid selling
online, 10
length of titles, 35-36
lens quality in digital
cameras, 45
lids, packing, 167
light boxes. *See* light tents
light tents, selecting, 49-50, 53
lighting
avoiding glare, 56
for photos, 46-48, 52-53
of clothing, 58-59
of opaque glass and
jewelry, 58
of translucent glass, 57
of wood items, 58
Lilly's Craft Stores Mall, 211
linking to Pinterest, 200-201
list price, 30
listing fees, 64
Artbreak, 66
Crobbies, 72
defined, 221
eBay, 79, 87, 117-118
Etsy, 65, 87, 97
Ruby Lane, 81
listings. *See* item listings
losses, profit versus, 29

M

macro mode (digital
cameras), 45
Made It Myself, 75
maintaining inventory levels,
181-182
managing
confirmation email
messages, 173
customer communications, 135
inventory. *See* inventory
management
item listings, 135
sales
on eBay, 129
on Etsy, 107-108
market analysis (in business
plan), 17
marketing services, 143
marketplaces. *See* online marketplaces
materials costs
calculating, 24
defined, 221
measuring. *See also* calculating
package size, 159
sales, 217-220
traffic, 214-217
membership fees
Artful Home, 68
Artist Rising, 69
mission statement (in business
plan), 17
models for clothing and
jewelry, 59
moiré patterns, 58
money orders, 107, 151
monthly fees
ArtFire, 67
Artspan, 69
Crobbies, 72
eBay Store, 127
Funky Finds, 72
Handmade Artists Shop, 73

Handmade Catalog, 74
Hyena Cart, 74
online shopping modules, 137
prepackaged storefronts, 137
Ruby Lane, 81
SilkFair, 82
site hosting, 137, 141
multiple photos of products, 55
multiple sites, selling on, 89
  benefits of, 183-184
  disadvantages of, 184-185
  inventory management,
    182, 185

N

navigation system, 135
net profit, calculating, 29, 223
news feed (Facebook), promotion via, 204

O

occasional sellers, business
  plans for, 13-14
online crafts malls, promotion
  with, 210-211
online marketplaces, 6-8
  linking to Pinterest, 200
  placement, 143
  selecting, 63
    comparison of sites, 83-84
    dedicated online craft mar-
      ketplaces, 64-77
    Etsy versus eBay, 86-88
    factors to consider, 84-86
    general online marketplaces,
      78-82
    multiple sites, 89, 183-185
online payments. *See* payment
  processing
online shopping modules, fees
  for, 137

opaque glass, photos of, 58
order processing services, 143
overhead, 25
own website. *See* ecommerce
  websites

P

package size, measuring, 159
packaging costs
  calculating, 25
  defined, 222
packing items
  how to pack a box, 165-166
  promotional materials, in-
    cluding, 110
  sealing package, 167-168
  shipping containers,
    selecting, 164
  tips for specific crafts, 166-167
Pages (Facebook), creating,
  205-206
pageviews, defined, 214
Parcel Post, 160
pay per click (PPC), 212
payment confirmation email
  message, 173
payment processing, 135
  fees for, 64, 138
    Craft is Art, 70
    defined, 221
    eBay, 129
    Etsy, 98, 106
    Yessy, 76
  methods for
    cash, 149
    cashier's checks, 151
    C.O.D., 149
    credit cards, 151-152
    on eBay, 129
    on Etsy, 105-107
    money orders, 151
    personal checks, 150
    pros and cons, 148

services, 143
  Checkout by Amazon,
    155-156
  Google Checkout, 154-155
  PayPal, 152-154
PayPal, 152-154
  on eBay, 129
  on Etsy, 106-107
The PayPal Official Insider
  Guide to Growing Your
  Business (Miller), 154
perishable items, selling
  online, 9
personal checks, 107, 150
personal style in item listings,
  40-41
personal website. *See*
  ecommerce websites
photo editing software
  selecting, 51
  what not to do, 52
photos
  of clothing, 58-59
  editing, 60-61
  equipment needed, 44-51
  in item listings, 41
  lighting, 52-53
  of opaque glass and
    jewelry, 58
  scanning items, 60
  tips for, 52-57
  of translucent glass, 57
  uploading
    to eBay, 132
    to Etsy, 103
  of wood items, 58
Pin It button, installing, 195
pinboards
  cover images, setting, 199
  customer-focused, 198-199
  explained, 192-193
  following, 193-194
pinning
  frequency of, 198
  item listings, 194-196

pins
  clicking, 190-192
  descriptive text, 200
  explained, 189-190
  as gift items, 196-198
  Pinterest, 187-189
    demographics, 188
    item listings, pinning, 194-196
    pinboards. *See* pinboards
    pins. *See* pins
    for promotion, 198-201
    signing up, 189
  Pinterest Follow button, installing, 200
planning. *See* business plans
plural words in titles, 34
post-sale email messages, managing, 173
power words
  in descriptions, 40
  in titles, 35
PPC (pay per click), 212
premade items
  custom made versus, 180-181
  maintaining inventory levels of, 181-182
prepackaged storefronts, 136-137
price. *See* selling price
price ranges on Pinterest, 198
printing shipping labels, 168-169
prioritizing item description information, 39
Priority Mail, 159
product pages, 135
product photos. *See* photos
product strategy (in business plan), 17
professional shipping stores, 162
profit, calculating, 29
  gross profit, 29, 220-222
  losses, 29
  net profit, 29, 223

profit margin, calculating, 222
promotion
  Etsy, 208-210
  Facebook, 204-206
  Google AdWords, 211-212
  online crafts malls, 210-211
  Pinterest, 198-201
  Twitter, 206-207
promotion strategy (in business plan), 18
promotional materials in packaging, 110
purchase confirmation email message, 173
Purolator Courier, 162

Q

questions
  answering
    from customers, 172
    in item descriptions, 37-39
  asking, when creating business plans, 15-17
QuickBooks integration, 144

R

refunds, offering, 176
registering
  for eBay account, 120
  for Etsy account, 98-99
renewing item listings in Etsy, 105
repinning, 192
reporting services, 144
requesting Pinterest invitations, 189
researching market, 22-23
reserve prices, defined, 119
resizing photos, 61
resolution of photos, 52, 61
retail pricing, wholesale pricing versus, 30
revenues, defined, 218

reviewing business plans, 20
risks section (in business plan), 18
Roberts, Pernell, 70
Ruby Lane, 81

S

sales, measuring, 217-220
  on eBay, 219-220
  on Etsy, 218-219
sales management
  on eBay, 129
  on Etsy, 107-108
Sales Reports Plus (on eBay), 128
Sams Teach Yourself Google Analytics in 10 Minutes (Miller), 217
scanning flat and small items, 60
sealing packages, 167-168
Search Ads in Etsy, 209-210
search advertising on Etsy, 96
search features, 135
searchable titles, writing, 33-34
selecting
  backgrounds for photography, 48-49
  categories on eBay, 130
  digital cameras, 44-45
  external lighting, 46-48
  hosting services, 141-146
  light tents, 49-50
  online marketplaces, 63
    comparison of sites, 83-84
    dedicated online craft marketplaces, 64-77
    Etsy versus eBay, 86-88
    factors to consider, 84-86
    general online marketplaces, 78-82
    multiple sites, 89, 183-185
  payment processing methods, 148-152

payment processing services, 152-156

photo editing software, 51

selling methods on eBay, 117

shipping containers, 164

shipping methods, 158-162

tripods, 46

self-run websites, 7. *See also* ecommerce websites

sellers, types on eBay, 113

selling fees, 64

Artbreak, 66

Artful Home, 68

Artist Rising, 69

Bonanza, 70

calculating, 25

Crobbies, 72

defined, 221

eBay, 79, 118

Etsy, 65, 97

Etsy versus eBay, 87

Made It Myself, 75

SilkFair, 82

Zibbet, 77

Selling Manager (on eBay), 128

selling methods on eBay

auction listings, 114-115

Buy It Now option, 115-116

fixed price listings, 116

selecting listing type, 117

Store listings, 116

selling price

calculating, 26-28

costs, calculating, 23-25

gross profit, calculating, 221

importance of, 12

researching market, 22-23

wholesale pricing, 30

ShipGooder, 158

shipping, what to avoid selling online, 8-10

shipping confirmation email message, 173

shipping containers, selecting, 164

shipping costs, 25

comparing, 158

insurance, 169

shipping fees, calculating, 104, 162-163

shipping labels, creating, 168-169

shipping methods

international shipping, 169

selecting, 158-162

shop (on Etsy)

creating, 100

customizing, 101-102

Shop Stats tool, 215

ShopHandmade, 76

shopping cart systems, 135, 142

shopping sites, types of, 6-7

signing up

eBay, 120

Etsy, 98-99

Pinterest, 189

SilkFair, 82

singular words in titles, 34

site design tools, 142

site hosting, 134

fees, 137, 141

selecting hosting services, 141-146

size of package, measuring, 159

size of websites, 85

small items, scanning, 60

social networks, linking to Pinterest, 201

soft boxes. *See* light tents

software for photo editing, 60-61

selecting, 51

what not to do, 52

speed lights, 47, 53

status updates (Facebook), promotion via, 204

Store listings on eBay, 116, 125-126

benefits of, 126

creating, 128

customizing, 128

fees, 127

setup, 128

storefronts. *See* ecommerce websites

subscription levels for eBay Store, 127

success, defining, 223-224

suggested retail price, 30

T

tags

defined, 104

importance of, 110

talking through business plans, 18-19

tape for sealing packages, 167-168

Terapeak website, 22

terms of service, listing, 175-176

The UPS Store, 162

tint, correcting in photos, 60

titles of item listings, writing, 32-36

TOS (terms of service), listing, 175-176

tracking. *See* calculating, measuring

tracking inventory. *See* inventory management

traffic on websites, measuring, 85

on eBay, 216

on Etsy, 215-216

on personal website, 216-217

web analytics, 214

transaction fees. *See also* selling
    fees
  Checkout by Amazon, 156
  Google Checkout, 155
  PayPal, 153
transactions, defined, 218
translucent glass, photos of, 57
tripods, selecting, 46
Twitter
  linking to Pinterest, 201
  promotion with, 206-207

U

United States Postal Service
    (USPS), 159-160
units sold, defined, 218
U-PIC, 169
uploading photos
  to eBay, 132
  to Etsy, 103
UPS, 161-162
The UPS Store, 162
Using Google AdWords and
    AdSense (Miller), 212
USPS (United States Postal
    Service), 159-160

V

vases, packing, 166
venues for selling crafts, 6-8
views, defined, 214
visitors, defined, 214

W

web analytics, 214
websites. *See also* online
    marketplaces
  auction sites, 7
  craft-focused, 6
  linking to Pinterest, 200
  self-run, 7

wholesale pricing, retail pricing
    versus, 30
wood items, photos of, 58
writing
  business plans, 20
  item listings, 31
    descriptions, 36-40
    personal style in, 40-41
    photos in, 41. *See also*
        photos
    titles, 32-36

Y

Yessy, 76
your website. *See* ecommerce
    websites

Z

Zibbet, 77
ZIP Code Finder, 168

Browse by Topic ▼ | Browse by Format ▼ | USING | More ▼

Store | Safari Books Online

QUEPUBLISHING.COM
Your Publisher for Home & Office Computing

Quepublishing.com includes all your favorite—and some new—Que series and authors to help you learn about computers and technology for the home, office, and business.

Looking for tips and tricks, video tutorials, articles and interviews, podcasts, and resources to make your life easier? Visit **quepublishing.com**.

- **Read the latest articles and sample chapters** by Que's expert authors

- **Free podcasts** provide information on the hottest tech topics

- **Register your Que products** and receive updates, supplemental content, and a coupon to be used on your next purchase

- **Check out promotions and special offers** available from Que and our retail partners

- **Join the site** and receive members-only offers and benefits

QUE NEWSLETTER
quepublishing.com/newsletter

 twitter.com/
quepublishing

 facebook.com/
quepublishing

 youtube.com/
quepublishing

 quepublishing.com/
rss

 Que Publishing is a publishing imprint of Pearson

SELLING YOUR CRAFTS ONLINE

with Etsy, eBay®, and Pinterest

MICHAEL MILLER

que

Safari
Books Online

FREE
Online Edition

Your purchase of *Selling Your Crafts Online* includes access to a free online edition for 45 days through the **Safari Books Online** subscription service. Nearly every Que book is available online through **Safari Books Online**, along with thousands of books and videos from publishers such as Addison-Wesley Professional, Cisco Press, Exam Cram, IBM Press, O'Reilly Media, Prentice Hall, Sams, and VMware Press.

Safari Books Online is a digital library providing searchable, on-demand access to thousands of technology, digital media, and professional development books and videos from leading publishers. With one monthly or yearly subscription price, you get unlimited access to learning tools and information on topics including mobile app and software development, tips and tricks on using your favorite gadgets, networking, project management, graphic design, and much more.

Activate your FREE Online Edition at
informit.com/safarifree

STEP 1: Enter the coupon code: JMFAYYG.

STEP 2: New Safari users, complete the brief registration form.
Safari subscribers, just log in.

If you have difficulty registering on Safari or accessing the online edition,
please e-mail customer-service@safaribooksonline.com

31901055270591